Self-Help, Personal Growth

THE WAY OF THE FOOL, THE WAY OF THE ABUNDANT FOOL
THE WAY OF THE IMPERFECT FOOL

It will transform your life!
REV. BRENDALYN BATCHELOR, UNITY SANTA FE

Simple but powerful!
DAVE KERPEN, AUTHOR OF "THE ART OF PEOPLE"

A transformational must-read!
LAURA DORFMAN, SALAMANCA, NY

Memoirs

ACTS OF SURRENDER: A WRITER'S MEMOIR
PILGRIMAGE: A FOOL'S JOURNEY
DIALOGUES WITH THE DIVINE: ENCOUNTERS WITH MY WISEST SELF

A dynamic read for the creative spirit
within each of us. Positive inspiration at its best.
HANK BRUCE, AUTHOR OF "PEACE BEYOND ALL FEAR:
A TRIBUTE TO JOHN DENVER'S VISION"

A book that has the power to awaken, empower
and inspire anyone who reads it.
MELISSA SHAWN, AUSTIN, TEXAS

Read it, love it, pass it on, and share Mark David's
gift with someone you love.
PAOLA RIZZATO, GLASGOW, UK

Resources for Writers

BOOKS, RECORDINGS, DOWNLOADABLE COURSES

Mark David Gerson is the best friend a writer ever had!
LUKE YANKEE, AUTHOR, PLAYWRIGHT AND SCREENWRITER

A highly recommended guide from
one of the most creative people around.
WILLIAM C. REICHARD, AUTHOR OF "EVERTIME"

Whenever I feel blocked, I open this book,
read a couple of pages and feel inspired again.
ANNA BLAGOSLAVOVA, MOSCOW, RUSSIA

Coaching, Counseling, Mentoring

Mark David Gerson is a master...one of the great teachers!
REV. MARY OMWAKE, UNITY OF MAUI

I owe so much to Mark David! He helped me believe in myself enough to write the book and do the public speaking that got two wrongful murder convictions overturned.
ESTELLE BLACKBURN, AUTHOR OF "BROKEN LIVES"

Mark David Gerson is a master teacher!
ELIZABETH HEARTSTAR, SEDONA, AZ

Mark David Gerson will make your book-writing dreams a reality. I know. He did it for me!
KAREN HELENE WALKER, AUTHOR OF "THE WISHING STEPS"

An amazing coach and mentor with a heart of love.
LEIA PHILIPS, SAN LEANDRO, CA

Even though I gave him no specifics, Mark David was able to intuit my situation and offer tremendous insight and inspiration. My time with him was incredibly helpful.
BLAINE JOHNSON, MINNEAPOLIS, MINNESOTA

Mark David Gerson helped me validate my intuition and make me feel that I have something to offer the world.
PROFESSOR CAROLE MACINNES, ACADIA UNIVERSITY

Fiction

THE LEGEND OF Q'NTANA VISIONARY FANTASIES
THE SARA STORIES SERIES

An exceptional, timeless novel.
"MINDQUEST REVIEW OF BOOKS"

Magic, music and universal truths masterfully woven into a gripping tale.
BETTY DRAVIS, AUTHOR OF "1106 GRAND BOULEVARD"

Gerson is a superb storyteller...I could not put it down!
"THE SUBURBAN," MONTREAL

Thrilling...bittersweet...triumphant!
DAN STONE, AUTHOR OF "ICE ON FIRE"

Writings Inspired by Melchizedek

The Book of Messages

Mark David Gerson

THE BOOK OF MESSAGES: WRITINGS INSPIRED BY
MELCHIZEDEK

Copyright © 2003, 2005, 2012, 2014, 2020 Mark David Gerson
All rights reserved

No part of this book may be reproduced, stored in a retrieval system or transmitted by any means, electronic, mechanical, photocopying, recording or otherwise, without written permission from the author, except for the inclusion of brief quotations in critical reviews and certain other noncommercial uses permitted by copyright law.

First Edition 2003
Second Edition 2014
Third Edition 2020

Published by MDG Media International
www.mdgmediainternational.com

ISBN: 978-1-950189-17-5 (print)
ISBN: 978-1-950189-18-2 (ebook)

Author Photograph: Kathleen Messmer
www.kathleenmessmer.com

Cover Photograph: Mark David Gerson

More information
www.markdavidgerson.com

*Where there is revelation, explanation
becomes superfluous.*
FREDERICK FRANCK

*Feel your fear, then pass through it to the other side,
where your destiny awaits.*
THE MOONQUEST

To the red rocks and transformative
energy of Sedona, where these words first
found me.

Contents

Foreword	9
Now Is the Time	19
1. You Have Been Chosen	23
2. You Are a Beacon	31
3. The Age of Synthesis	37
4. The Melchizedek Energies	47
5. Choose Fearlessness	53
6. Your Greatest Strength and Power	61
7. Celebrate Your Voice	69
8. The Mansion of Your Beingness	75
9. Choose Life	85
10. Your Rainbow Self	97
11. Speak Your Truth	105
12. Own Your Voice	113
13. Choose Empowerment	123
You and Melchizedek	135
Free Your Melchizedek Energies onto the Page	139
Step into Your Melchizedek Energy: A Guided Meditation	143
Gratitude	149
More from Mark David Gerson	153
Be the Melchizedek You Are!	164

Foreword

Each time I revisit *The Book of Messages,* no matter how many years have passed since my previous reading, I am startled to discover how current its words still are — in my life as much as in the world.

At this writing, fear has so permeated the political culture of so many nations that it can feel some days as though we are plummeting into the hellish depths of darkness instead of skyrocketing toward the light of Ascension. That makes these messages even more relevant now than they were seventeen years ago when the first of them crept up on me just after dawn on a crisp November morning.

Yet, as I was reminded that morning and as these thirteen messages remind me still, no matter how dark the preceding night, the sun always rises on a new day. They remind me, too, that we are the architects of our own destinies and that when we shatter the illusion of duality and free ourselves to move through and past our fears and perceived limitations, anything is possible.

Anything *is* possible. I have experienced the truth of that more times and in more ways than I can enumerate here, and each reading of *The Book of Messages* reminds me of that. That's because as much as this book is for you, its messages still speak powerfully to me.

Through this most recent reading, as I prepare

Messages for a new edition, I have once again been amazed that its principle themes are as true to my life as ever — themes that remind me to empower myself, celebrate my voice, choose fearlessness and honor my inner diversity.

Perhaps the most compelling reminder of all, though, is the book's call to "re-member": to bring back into wholeness all the scattered parts of myself...to reattach all the severed limbs of my beingness...to reweave all the loose threads of my story into a single tapestry.

Two of my books, *Acts of Surrender: A Writer's Memoir* and *The SunQuest*, the third story in my *Legend of Q'ntana* fantasy series, also speak eloquently to those themes. By its nature, a memoir is a form of synthesis that forces its author to carry out the kind of re-membering called for in nearly every one of this book's messages. Writing the Ben character in *The SunQuest* forced me onto a similar, if less direct journey.

In a curious twist of synchronicity, I recently reread both *Acts of Surrender* and *The SunQuest*; this, before I knew that I would be preparing this new *Messages* edition. Six years ago, the ink was barely dry on both *Acts of Surrender* and *The SunQuest* when I was getting *The Book of Messages* ready for its then-new edition. Books, including our own, always show up when we most need them.

In that earlier edition's foreword, I remarked how both books had forced me to own *all* my "ages and stages," especially ones, like the original *Book of Messages* period in my life, that I had considered to be no longer relevant.

Why had I come to view the *Book of Messages* period in my life as irrelevant? In my mind, I had shut the door on Sedona when I moved away in 2004 and on my overtly metaphysical persona a few years later when I refocused my writing and teaching in more mainstream directions.

I hadn't shut any doors, of course. As *A Wrinkle in Time* author Madeleine L'Engle so eloquently put it, "I am still every age that I have been." That was one of the reasons why in 2014 I felt called to bring *The Book of Messages* back into print.

Then, I was living in Albuquerque. Today, to my astonishment, I find myself not only back in Sedona but less than a mile from the scrubby, red-rock trail where the first of these messages came to me.

If that weren't "re-membering" enough, in returning to Sedona, my first home in this country, I have come back to my US roots, which makes my presence here another act of whole-making.

For many reasons, then, this is the perfect moment in my life to not only revisit *The Book of Messages* — both its timeless contents and its significance to my own journey — but to share a new edition with you.

Where did these Messages come from? You'll find answers to that question in my "Foreword to the First Edition," which follows in a few pages, and in the "Changing Channels" excerpt from my *Acts of Surrender* memoir at the back of the book.

Finally, I daren't conclude this Foreword without addressing another question that I know some of you are already posing: Who or what is Melchizedek?

I promise you the beginnings of an answer once you have read Message #1 and more clarity still once you have finished Message #4. If you choose, you can have a direct Melchizedek experience of your own in "You and Melchizedek," which follows Message #13, and in that chapter's guided meditation, "Step into Your Melchizedek Energy."

In short, though, the Biblical Melchizedek was a king and priest who first appeared to Abraham in Genesis. In metaphysical circles, he symbolizes a powerful source of ancient wisdom. In *The Book of Messages*, though, he's much, much more. Read on and you'll see!

Sedona, Arizona
January 2020

Foreword to the First Edition

This book is a compilation of inspirational writings that began to move through me soon after I returned to Sedona, Arizona after three and a half years living in Hawaii.

One of Sedona's treasures is the thousands of acres of publicly accessible Forest Service land that surround and insinuate itself into this Northern Arizona community. You can, as I do many days, step out your door and onto land that has changed little over the centuries. It's an elemental experience of connectedness that continues to touch me deeply and rarely fails to return me to center.

It's also an experience that was largely absent during my time on the Big Island and Maui, where most of the open, non-beach land is privately owned and closed to public use.

So when I returned to Sedona, one of the first things I did was instigate a morning ritual of meditative nature walks among the cactus, mesquite and juniper of this mystical high-desert country.

As I walked, most days, powerful messages of hope, inspiration and en-courage-ment began to move through me, messages that guided and reassured me and helped fortify me for my day.

In the beginning, no particular name or energy attached itself to the words. After a time, however, the name Melchizedek suggested itself as their source.

Messages such as these were not new for me. I

had written many over the years. What was new was speaking them aloud. Also new was the impetus to record, transcribe and share them.

It took several weeks to build up the courage to send the first message out. I titled it "Message from Melchizedek" and, in November 2002, emailed it to a selection of friends, clients and students, encouraging them to pass it on.

Within two days, I had received more than forty requests to be added to the mailing list, all from strangers.

Now, five months and a dozen messages later, more than six hundred people in some twenty-five countries are receiving these occasional mailings. Countless others are reading them on my website or on the other sites on which they appear.

No one has been more amazed than I!

It is this response that has prompted me to make these messages available in a more durable and convenient form.

Why are they no longer titled "Messages from Melchizedek"? You'll find the full answer in Messages #12 and #13. Those messages address in great depth and detail how important it is to integrate all the loving energies that work with us and move through us and to claim them as part of our beingness.

In brief, the same Melchizedek energies that sparked all these outpourings challenged me to empower myself and my voice by claiming the words as my own.

Therefore, although inspired by Melchizedek, these are "Messages from my Wisest Self[1]." I take responsibility for them and lovingly share them with you.

---

[1] "Wisest Self" is my preferred term for what some refer to as "Higher Self."

May they contribute as much to your empowerment and transformation as they have to mine.

Sedona, Arizona
April 2003

Now Is the Time...

We live in times of radical transformation. Whatever seemed fixed and certain in the past is now breaking apart as you and I and all who dwell on this planet face choices that seemed inconceivable a few years ago.

Will we continue to live in the fear-based culture we have created through thousand of lifetimes? Or will we move into the higher frequencies and vibrations of the Heaven on Earth our souls yearn for?

Will we continue to live through our ego/personality self? Or will we surrender to the Divinity of the God Self that longs to live through us in the physical realm?

Now is the time to integrate all that you are and embrace the full wisdom of your highest and Wisest Self. Now is the time to quicken the self-transformation that is already moving through you.

Now is the time.

1. You Have Been Chosen

You have been chosen. You have been chosen and you chose.

You chose the Melchizedek whole-making journey, just as you were chosen for it.

You agreed many, many, many, many lifetimes ago to return to this time — at the End Times which are also the New Times — to assist with and hasten The Change.

Yes, the entire Universe experiences this Change now — one that was foretold by the Ancients, one you knew was imminent when you chose to be part of the vanguard team that would hasten and accelerate its arrival, that would ease and lubricate its effecting and implementation.

You were chosen and you chose. You chose to separate yourself from the Mass Consciousness so you could change, transform and revolutionize it.

You didn't pull away from mass consciousness because *you* didn't fit in. You pulled away because *it* didn't fit in. It didn't fit in with the Cosmic Plan for Universal Transformation, one for which you as a Melchizedek helped draw the blueprints and are now here as part of the Activation Team.

Yes, you carry Melchizedek energy. If you are reading this and resonating with this, if you have ever felt curiosity about Melchizedek or the Order of Melchizedek, if you have ever wondered how you could join this Order or whether you already were a member, then you carry Melchizedek energy. You are simply in the re-membering process as you reintegrate that sacred, ancient energy, choice and beingness back into your conscious awareness.

What does all this mean? What does it mean to carry Melchizedek energy? What does it mean to be part of the Activation Team? For now, know that it means many things, for there is not just one way in which you are called to act. There are many. Many with meaning.

Allow yourself to remember them, to reclaim them, to surrender to them, to release into them. Let your reluctance dissolve, for it has no place at this time or in these times.

Your reluctance is borne of forgetfulness. You forget who you are, what you are, why you are here and why it is so critical that you do remember — more fully than all that you do remember and have remembered to this point.

Remember who you are and what you are. You are a mighty Priest Most High, a member of a mighty order Most High. If you read this and resonate to it, if you read this and have *any* emotional response (even anger or fierce denial), *you are a priest of the Most High Order of Melchizedek*. Whether you feel ready to read this or know it, it is true.

Long ago were you ordained, so long ago that the memory of the actual act is as the mists rising from a lake. Ages ago did you choose and agree to help with this Change — which is a change in you as much as it is a change in the very energetic fabric of the cosmos.

For you who read this, your soul's highest choice (as it was your soul's highest desire and choice to seek out your original Melchizedek commitment and to seek out, in this lifetime, your renewal and re-membering of that choice) is to honor the Holy Trinity of your calling, which is the calling of all Melchizedeks, to one degree and extent or another:

Writing
Teaching
Whole-making

Every Melchizedek will have different emphases placed on each of these components, a different soul emphasis and different emphases at different parts and times in each incarnation.

It is for each of you reading this to discern the balance for you, *knowing* that whichever element elicits fear or resistance at this moment in time is the element upon which you are called to place the greater part of your will and love, in order to melt, dissolve and eradicate your resistance — not solely for your whole-making but for the world's.

Are you not writing? Then write, for a Melchizedek is also a record-keeper, a keeper not only of the past and present record but, most important still, of the future record.

What you write is less a journaling of thoughts, feelings and emotions past (as transitionally transformational as that can be) as an imprinting of what is to be — this, as much through the energy of your words set to print as through their content.

Whether you are clear, at this moment, about what you see and "know," you *are* a prophet and visionary

— not predicting *an* outcome so much as visioning the array of outcomes, all of which are simultaneously present and possible.

You see it, and whether you know it consciously or not, your words reflect it, carry the energy of it.

You are an energy worker in all you do, and your words carry powerful energy.

So, write.

For your writings — completed, contemplated and in progress — are key elements in your mission, calling and prearranged choice. Remember that.

Now, to teaching.

Melchizedeks are teachers as well as priests. Priests, like rabbis, are, first and foremost, teachers.

You are not an intermediary to Spirit, as many in the traditional Christian teaching have mistakenly come, over the millennia, to characterize themselves. You are a link. There is a difference. An intermediary believes him/herself to be an ever-necessary connection point to the Divine, on the false assumption that most people cannot, will not or should not have a direct experience of the Divine.

A link is a guide, opening individuals to their own divinity and reconnecting them to the oneness that is the only truth, the only All That Is...leading individuals into their *own* power and empowerment, which is their own recognition and experience of The Source of All within each of them.

The teaching element can be accomplished and effected in many ways that are not mutually exclusive and that differ for each individual. None may involve standing before a class in a formal setting. All involve a public form of communication, a public voicing of truths, a public opening of your throat chakra through speech. Be open to the way(s) this part of your mission will manifest for you.

A critical part of your teaching path is teaching-through-being. Being the Melchizedek you are — openly, lovingly and heartfully — is, itself, a powerful teaching. So be all that you would teach and re-member, and this critically important part of your choice and mission will take care of itself.

And, now to whole-making...

You are one who makes whole. You do it through your words and your teaching. But as a Melchizedek, are you called to a more direct experience and expression of the whole-making process.

Look at your hands and know that. Feel, however faintly, the energy flowing from Spirit through your hands. *That energy is needed right now.*

Right now, in this instant. And right now, in *this* now.

Do not run from the power which is so much a part of you, so integral to who and what you are.

It is part of your whole-making as an individual and part of the cosmic whole-making you chose and were chosen to assist with, a cosmic whole-making of the entire beingness and oneness of Spirit, in all its dimensions and manifestations.

Of course, these roles — writing, teaching, whole-making — are not mutually exclusive. Each is a part of the others and all work together in a harmonious oneness, when you let them, when you surrender to them and allow...when you surrender to your Melchizedekness and trust in the power for infinite good and cosmic healing and whole-making that has rested in you for so long that it is part of the essence of who and what you are.

And so, yes, your writing is a teaching and whole-making. Your whole-making is a teaching. Your teaching is a whole-making. But do not ignore or diminish these elements in their individuality, for they are critical — to your Melchizedek journey of wholeness and to your Melchizedek journey of cosmic whole-making.

That is all for now.

Finally, this blessing...

May the opening you now feel in your heart blossom and expand until it reaches, touches and embraces every other heart and heart energy in the cosmos — friend and perceived foe alike, priest and terrorist alike.

For only in that embrace will oneness return to the cosmos, as it must if Heaven on Earth is to be attained and achieved in this lifetime — in your lifetime.

Your whole-making is in progress. Join it consciously, if you have not already, through an act of love and oneness today, as you acknowledge, embrace and live the fullness of your Melchizedek beingness.

Blessings to you all — now and forever more.

2. You Are a Beacon

Greetings, my friend. Greetings and blessings on this wondrous day of light...your light.

You are a Way-Shower. You are a Way-Shower of the light. And your role, among others right now, wherever you live, is to hold that light.

But it is also to show that light and speak that light.

There are others of light where you live who are not yet capable of openly holding that light. They are not as strong as you are. They are not as courageous as you are...yet.

It can feel frightening, particularly in a place where it seems there are no other lightworkers, where it seems there is no light, to be the lightworker you are, to be it in an open way. But how will there be other lightworkers with the courage to open to the light within them if there is no model for them? That is what a Way-Shower does and is: models the light, models the way.

So breathe into the Way-Shower you are, the lightshower you are, the light that you are.

It is so important in these times that everywhere, in every community, there is at least one being — one beam — of light to shine into what seems like darkness but is only fear.

You are not alone where you live...although perhaps

you are alone in your courage. Perhaps you are alone in the brightness, in this moment of your light.

Everywhere around you there is light, waiting to be kindled, waiting for permission to blossom, to open like a lotus. So open to that light within yourself and allow it to shine in a way that perhaps you have not fully allowed yourself, yet.

To whatever extent you have allowed it to shine, and know that you have, it is time to amp up the energy of that, to brighten the light of that.

You are a beacon. You know that. You are a beacon and a lighthouse whose beam, whose golden ray, helps make it safe for other sailors in these sometimes, seemingly harsh seas.

Allow them to see your light. Allow those who perhaps you don't consciously know to feel this light. Allow them to see your light in the courage that you possess, letting go all the lifetimes where being this light has been problematic. Because in this moment, in *this* moment, all that can be gone. For all time is now.

Close your eyes. Clap you hands with the force of your choice. Clap your hands and everything is clear. Every lifetime is clear. Every dimension is clear. Every part of your beingness that holds that fear of what will happen to you if you shine your light in a public way is gone.

Clap again.

And again.

It is gone, gone as though it never existed. For, in truth, it never did.

So breathe into the beacon of light that you are, and see it grow brighter and brighter and brighter, connecting with other beacons of light and forming a grid

The Book of Messages

of light — consciously forming a grid of light that circles the Earth and expands out into the cosmos.

You are a key point in this grid *where you are in this moment*. That does not mean that where you are in this moment is forever. But where you are in this moment, you are a key part of the grid.

And as a magnet, you draw to you all those other beings, those reluctant beams, those wavering flames, those not-quite-lit matches in your very community.

Allow them to come to you. Create ways in which they can see your light and know that it is safe. For as unsafe as those parts of you feel that it is, can you imagine how unsafe it feels to all those who can't even begin to light their light a fraction of what you have done?

Allow your light to shine and draw them into you. Draw them into you that you might, without being parasitically fed off, feed their flame. Through feeding their flame, you will feed your own. Through feeding their passion, you will feed your own. Through feeding their light and life, you will feed your own.

Then you will have created and anchored, in truth, the light where you are. You will have anchored the light where *you* are. Earthwork, working with the Earth grids, is part of that anchoring. But anchoring is more than earthwork. It is people-work.

For it is people who walk the earth. It is people whose light affects the light of the Earth, and vice-versa. So breathe into the knowingness that you are a powerful, powerful, powerful being *and* beam of light...a magnetic being and beam of light that can draw to you and to where you are all the other beings and beams of life that can help anchor — truly, truly anchor — the light where you are.

That is *so* important in these times, in these times of change, in these times of synthesis, in these times of coming back together, of re-membering, re-attaching all that has been severed and seemingly forgotten. It is important that everywhere there is at least one bearer of the torch, one Way-Shower of the light.

Where you are, you are one of those. And it is an important role, a key role.

There is fear. Of course, there is fear. Choose, in those moments of fear, to love — to love even the fear, to love even the parts of you that are in fear. Through that love, dissolve the fear and choose another way... choose to move forward as the light that you are.

There are many Way-Showers; you are one. A powerful such one. Honor that role that *you* have chosen. Honor it and be of it.

Be the beacon you are, the lighthouse you are. Let your powerful beam of courage, fearlessness and open-heartedness, of gold and platinum light, shine from the core of your beingness out into the world — filling the room in which you sit, the town in which you dwell, the country you call home, the continent that anchors it, the planet that relies on you and the cosmos that is the infinite All That Is.

Your light matters. Let it shine.

Move into the rest of your day, now, with this blessing:

May your light join with all lights in a powerful ray
of whole-making that illuminates all that is in the
openness and courage of your true heart.

Blessings to you, my friend. Abundant and light-filled blessings.

3. The Age of Synthesis

Greetings, my friend. Greetings and welcome to this wondrous time. We enter, to repeat from an earlier message, the Age of Synthesis. This is the great time of coming together back into oneness. This is the time of reweaving all the disparate parts of yourself, and of the cosmos, together in a Great Godhead Oneness from which we all emerged.

But there is a difference now. Just as each of you has a body characterized by arms and legs, a nose, a mouth, eyes, teeth, hair, wrinkles — all of which are individual elements coming together to form a whole — so is the Body Cosmic.

The Body Cosmic, too, is an entity, a body made up of individual beings. So as you move back into the oneness from which you emerged, you move back as an individual expressions of that oneness.

What a more beautiful image than just one, perhaps, glob of godliness!

How much better, as we synthesize, to move back into these wondrous individual expressions, all part of a great and growing and magnificent oneness, but each an individual expression. Here, an arm, there a leg. Here, a musician, there an artist. Here, a healer, there a teacher. All coming together in a Great Body Cosmic that already exists.

What is truly coming together now is the awareness of that Great Body Cosmic.

This is the Age of Synthesis. This is the age of coming back together again, of reweaving all the disparate parts that make up this Body Cosmic.

To say "all the disparate parts," means all those parts of you that you have disowned. All those parts of you that lie unloved. All those parts of you, light *and* dark, that lie in the shadow, under the covers, under the bed... hidden away in a deep, dark recess of the closet.

It is time to embrace the *fullness* of who you are, and in so doing, the great cosmic oneness, the great cosmic unity, the great Body Cosmic comes together through *you*.

This is the time of synthesis, the Great Time — not so much of change, for change suggests that what you are will somehow shift or transform. This is the time of Re-Membering.

It is time to bring back each "member" of the being that you are — each member, as in a limb, as in each limb that has been severed. It is time to bring it back, to reattach it, to re-*member* it — calling back, like a shepherd who calls lost sheep in his flock, all those parts of you that you have denied, that you have said aren't good enough, that you have believed aren't spiritual enough.

You cannot leave anything behind, for there is no end to any piece of energy. So it is not about leaving behind. It is about transmuting.

It is about taking those parts of you that are not fully whole and bringing them back into consciousness, that they may be re-membered, reattached, re-healed and re-wholed...wholed, as in making whole.

This is the Age of Synthesis, of Whole-Making. The age of pulling apart is over. It is done. It is complete.

This is the Age of Re-Membering, of reattaching, of re-newing.

Go into your closet. Look under your bed. Check out the dark recesses of your consciousness. What have you denied? What have you not allowed to surface because you think it is ugly? Because it frightens you? Because you believe you already left it behind and don't want to see it again? What is it in your consciousness, what is it in your life, that you are not noticing, recognizing, acknowledging and, yes, even embracing?

Bring them all back into the light, for in the light will they be healed and will they be made whole...will *you* be made whole.

This is about taking the wondrous tapestry that you are, that wondrous tapestry of disparate threads, and reweaving it back into the wholeness that is the oneness of you...the oneness of all your lifetimes, of all the dimensions in which you now dwell, of all the planes and planets and times and elements of space in which you dwell.

You dwell in all of them in this moment, of course, for there is no such thing as time — past, present or future. All time is now.

In reweaving this now, all is healed and made whole *now*. And what occurred four thousand lifetimes ago, or what occurs in this moment in another plane of existence, in another dimension, is healed, *in this moment*. For all moments are now.

Imagine a tapestry, a wonderful symbol of the oneness that you are. Look at it, in your mind's eye. Imagine pulling threads out that somehow don't look good to you. Pull out too many threads and the whole wondrous piece of work begins to unravel, begins to look frayed and shabby.

So take all those threads that have become unraveled or that you have pulled free from the tapestry and reweave and reinsert those golden threads of your beingness back into the tapestry. Pull each thread off the floor, out of the closet, out of the deep, dark basement of your sewing kit. Hold it in your hand. Acknowledge it. Love it. Watch it transform.

You have an ugly side to your nature? Who does not. Acknowledge it. See within you where it is and what triggers it. Choose otherwise, and in that choice-making you have transmuted that old thread and turned it into a brilliant new gold one, ready to be reinserted into your tapestry of wholeness and oneness and life.

Then as each tapestry becomes whole again, are these tapestries woven together into the great cosmic tapestry, which, of course, already exists, but is repaired in this act.

This is the great time of synthesis. This *is* the Change. This is the time of moving into oneness and wholeness. This is the light that you are. So embrace all of you.

When you are done embracing all of you, embrace all of your neighbor. And when you are done embracing the fullness of the tapestry of your neighbor, embrace the tapestry of your friend. And then, of your enemy. For we are all one in this cosmic tapestry. And until we embrace each and every thread and strand of the tapestry, we cannot acknowledge and transmute those threads that are no longer serving us.

It is not about pulling threads out and throwing

them away. It is about transforming the threads that already exist. For all is energy. And energy cannot be created or destroyed. It already and always exists.

Pulling those rotten or ugly threads, as you might term them, out of the tapestry and throwing them into the back of your closet does not destroy them. It leaves them there to fester, to mold, to mildew, to become even uglier out of the light of the sun, out of the light of the day.

So embrace them. Embrace them, and in embracing them, see them change. Allow them to change. Allow yourself to change through them and them to change through you.

This *is* the Age of Synthesis. Welcome it. Embrace it. Be it. Play with it. Be of it. And see the Heaven on Earth, which is the great cosmic tapestry, come into consciousness. See it emerge — triumphant, resplendent — a heavenly creation finally acknowledged by you, its creator as the beautiful thing it is, the beautiful thing you are...the beautiful thing *all* are.

Many come bearing many different messages, and each of these messages, coming from a place of loving consciousness, is a powerful part of the whole, of the cosmic tapestry, of the Body Cosmic.

Allow your discernment to work with each of these messages — this one as well as any one you hear from anywhere, so that you know in your heart which is true for you. For there are many wondrous lights beaming amazing, grace-filled messages of hope and joy and courage at this time.

At this time, too, there are many who appear as lights, who think in their ego-minds that they are lights, yet whose messages are tinged with fear, are cracked with judgment and are broadcast from a place of un-wholeness.

So open your heart. Allow your heart to filter all that comes to you and through you, including this very message. For some messages are of the light and some at this time are not. Some messages, even that are of the light, are not right for you at this time but may be at a later date. And some messengers who appear unwhole today may return to wholeness, and their messages may shift.

So be open to all. The potential for light exists in *everyone*. It exists in what some might term the saint and what some might term the sinner. It exists, too, in what some might term the terrorist or the sniper. It exists in the political leader you never voted for and wish nobody had. It exists in those who voted for him or her. It exists in all. By opening to those threads within our tapestry which we have rejected, we create an opening for all to do likewise, including those you might term sinner or terrorist, including that political leader.

Every heart opened creates an opening for a thousand hearts to open, tens of thousands of hearts to open. Every thread that is renewed and restored and rewoven into the fabric of your beingness creates an opening for other threads in other beings in other tapestries, as all come together in the great cosmic tapestry, the great cosmic body that is the oneness that is All That Is.

Open your heart. Open your mind. Open your eyes. See and feel and know and touch the beauty of that tapestry — the beauty it is *in this moment*, in spite of the missing threads, in spite of the frayed threads, in spite of the wrong color placed here or there. *It is beautiful in this moment.* It will be rendered yet more beautiful still as you embrace, in love, all those threads, all those parts of your body spiritual, body physical and body emotional that you would prefer, in moments, not be present.

Allow yourself to become whole again. Allow yourself to become one again. Allow yourself to be the divinity you are again.

This is the Age of Synthesis. Bring all of you back together again. Bring all the parts of you back together again. Then bring all the beings with those parts back together again. Do this now. Do this now.

These are wondrous times. These are joy-filled times. These are times of miraculous healing and whole-making for you, for your nation, for your planet, for the Universe and for the cosmos. Be a conscious part of that.

Be a conscious part of that and see, with your physical eyes and your divine heart, the transformations, the divinity that spreads and enlarges, the Heaven on Earth of the Age of Synthesis you have been promised.

See all that unfold in your lifetime, beginning with this breath, beginning today, beginning now. Blessings to you, my friend.

Blessings of great love, of great abundance, of great whole-making and of great light.

4. The Melchizedek Energies

In the beginning was total oneness. There was no differentiation, no individuation, no individuals — simply the One, which, for convenience only, can be called God.

Forget other versions of this story. All versions are true, in their own way. This is the one that matters in this moment.

In what you might call God's loneliness, It created. Not from nothingness but from Itself.

Like an amoeba, It began to split off parts of Itself into other whole beings. These were beings of independent immediate destinies, even if their ultimate destiny was already written: to return, ultimately, to the oneness, enriched by their experiences of individuality...to return to the oneness as the tapestry spoken of in Message #3.

All are part of that oneness, that creative splitting off.

The Melchizedek energies, too, were part of that splitting off. And they emerged with a distinct task: To ensure that all the beings split off from the Godhead had souls. The job description, if you will, revolves around directing the "ensouling" of the Universe.

Melchizedek energies were present, at God's right hand, for the splitting off and individuation. And there they remain, directing the return to Source as all the souls come back together again — not in an amorphous, homogenized "glob," but as wondrous stars in a giant constellation of wholeness and oneness.

These energies are present in your life to communicate to you and through you the means and assists that will allow all souls split apart in what was then a giant, untested experiment to return — not to their former undifferentiated state, but to a new, untested state of unity in diversity, of wholeness in individuation.

These energies come to you and reawaken within you in many different guises and with many linked messages. The point is always the same: The return to oneness, the return to wholeness, the return to love. For it was from love that you emerged and it is to love that you will return.

At some level, all know the Melchizedek energy, for all new souls pass through it before traveling into the density to become embodied. All know these energies, but most have forgotten them.

This is fine. Melchizedek energies exist not to be remembered but to help others to remember themselves. They exist to help *you* remember yourself, to recall the Great Soul that is the true directing force of your beingness and purpose.

These energies are being rekindled and reawakened within you to assist you as you empower yourself to recognize and live the fullness of your potential in all manner and in all ways, so that when the great Coming Together is complete, you are not subsumed or submerged in an amorphous oneness. Instead, you stand fully realized and empowered, an integral, individual thread in a vast tapestry.

Let these energies awaken within you. Allow them a key role in your re-membering, reawakening and re-wholing. Remember who you are, all of who you are. And allow the Melchizedek energies long dormant within you to explode in a multicolored, multidimensional, multifaceted rainbow of oneness...the oneness you are.

Be the loving, transformational, whole-making energy that you are. Honor it. Celebrate it. Act upon it.

Blessings to you — on your day and on your whole-making.

5. Choose Fearlessness

Blessings to you, my friend. Blessings and greetings from Sedona on this fine day. Your heavenly heart smiles within you with great joy this day. For you launch yourself yet more fully on your journey of awakening and re-membering.

Step forward, step by step. And as you step more fully into that oneness in your own heart, then will you come closer to your divinity, if that is your chosen destiny.

Step by step by step. That is the key. Step by step by step.

Do not doubt. Do not hesitate. Do not let fear interrupt your journey.

Acknowledge the fear, for fear is human. But the journey is Divine, and you cannot permit the fear to interrupt your journey toward divinity. You who have carried so much fear in you over so many lifetimes that it is fully embedded in your cellular structure must now fully release its power over you.

Choose to release its power over you. Let the fear be. Let it have its life. But let it not be a life that destroys your own.

Breathe out the fear. Breathe it out and let it go. And *know* that no fear is stronger than you are. No fear is more powerful than you are. No fear is more courageous than you are. No fear can stand in your way, unless you choose to allow it that freedom.

Take back the keys of the city. Take back the keys of the city that have allowed fear to run free in your life.

There is no room for it now. There is no space for it now. There is no need for it now. For all the fear you have carried through all these lifetimes, through all these dimensions, through all these realms, is obsolete.

It cannot protect you any longer.

The fear was designed to protect you. It can no longer protect you. It does no longer protect you. That is not its purpose and function anymore. All it does right now is stop and delay you.

In stopping and delaying you, it does the opposite of protect you. Yes, it feels like protection. It feels like, "If I give in to this fear, I will be safe or safer." But no, dear friend. No. That is no longer the case.

The key here is to acknowledge, to "grok," if you will, the concept that fear does not, cannot, will not protect you any longer.

Of course, it did at one time. Of course, it was important in your history and prehistory. Of course, the fear made you run away from danger.

Now the fear makes you run away from your safety.

Your safety, your physical, emotional, spiritual and divine safety, lies not in the direction of your fear.

Fear carries you *away* from the light, the brightness, the joy, the passion. Fear stops you from realizing that light, that brightness, that joy, that passion.

Your fear is not the enemy. It is not even the adversary. For there are no enemies or adversaries in this way of being, in this way of doing, in this dimension into which you now move.

Your fear is an old friend that is now holding you back. We have all had embodied individuals in our lives who have said "don't" — not because they were afraid for you but because they were afraid for themselves.

You fear says "don't" — not any longer because it is afraid for you. It is afraid for itself.

So speak to your fear. Speak to your fear and find out how your fear can transform into discernment. Speak to your fear and find out how your fear can grow into wisdom.

Choose discernment and wisdom that your fear might not block your steps into the light, into wholeness and full beingness. Choose discernment and wisdom that *they* might stop you from stepping back, running away, dis-acknowledging your power — dis-acknowledging who and what you truly are. That *is* what your fear does now.

Do not allow — *for you are in charge* — your fear to say "no" to you. Allow your discernment to say "no," but do not allow your fear to say "no" to you. Your fear will. Your fear, to repeat, is based upon lifetimes upon lifetimes upon lifetimes of real dangers that you wanted to run from, that you needed to run from.

Yes, you needed to run from the wild animals. Yes, you needed to run from the predators. Yes, your fear created in you the physical response that allowed you to do that. That was good. That was important. That was, in fact, critical to your very survival.

Now, fear is antithetical to your survival. Fear will, in fact, hasten your demise in a spiritual sense and, perhaps, even in a physical sense.

Fear's time has passed. Now is the time to be fearless. And when fearlessness does not seem possible, it is the time to be so steeped in courage that the brilliant light of that courage overtakes the fear, drowns it out, swamps it, melts it and dissolves it.

This refers both to courage before *and* courage after the act. For, in some cases, the fear does not hit, if you will, until after the act of the courage.

Do not let your fear stand in *your* way any longer, for, to repeat, fear is an obsolete emotion. Fear is a hindrance. It is no longer a helper. It is a destroyer, not a protector.

This is not about casting off parts of yourself. Fear is not a part of yourself. Fear is the expression of a part of yourself. That part of yourself needs to find a new expression.

Ask that part of yourself that is now that embodiment of the fear:

- How can I help you to help me to move forward in love?
- How can I help you to help me to move forward in light?
- How can I help you to help me to move forward on my soul's path of whole-makingness and beingness?
- How can I help you to help me, for I need the help of all parts of me?
- Yes, I need your help. But I need it in a new way. I need it in a way that is *not* fear-based.

That is the key to this Message.

Previous Messages have spoken of this Age of Synthesis, an age of not tossing out old parts of you. All those parts of you are the foundation upon which the new has been created. So if you rip out the foundation, you rip out the very basis upon which you now stand. Not a helpful thing.

Embrace all parts of you. But ask those parts of you that are holding emotions, responses and reactions that are now hurtful, harmful, damaging and *anything but protective* to help you by helping them to find a new way. Choose that new way — for all parts of yourself.

You are all that you have ever been in every lifetime, in every dimension, on every plane of existence. You need all those parts of you.

You can let the past go — that is, let go the emotions of the past, the perceived errors of the past. But every part of you, every age you have ever been, every age in which you have ever lived, is still within you. It cannot be cast off and should not be cast off and must not be cast off.

It is there to assist you. It is there as the very basis of who you have become — for lifetime after lifetime after lifetime. Through those lifetimes you have grown into this. You have opened your heart, transformed your life and grown closer to the Godhead from which you were separated.

Once again — and again and again and again — fear served you well for many, many millennia. But its time has passed. And so you must let it pass. *Choose* to let it pass.

Address that part of you that holds that response within it. Love it into knowing that fear is no longer a necessary, helpful or protective response.

Perhaps there is more than one part of you that calls out to be addressed. Take it one part at a time. One day at a time. Today and again tomorrow and again next week, perhaps, if that is necessary.

In each moment, in every moment, choose to open to your heart, reawaken your fearlessness and reintegrate your power. Use your discernment in each moment to help you make those choices.

Choose fearlessness. Choose discernment. Choose empowerment. Choose love — for all parts of yourself and for all humanity. Choose it.

Choose it now.

You are loved. You are love. And all is well.

6. Your Greatest Strength and Power

Greetings and blessings on this beloved day, on this day of the Beloved that *you* are, which is every day that you open to your greater power, your greater light, your greater courage and your greater love.

This is such a day, for each day that you connect with your Greater Self is such a day.

And so, blessings.

You know you are an important Presence. Acknowledge that yet more deeply.

You have changed lives. You do change lives. Acknowledge that, too.

Know, too, that through *all* you do through your connection with your highest power and empowerment, your highest self and your God Self, you are effecting the transformation you came here to effect. You effect it within yourself and you help midwife it within all others with whom you come into contact.

Celebrate that on this wondrous day. Celebrate it and acknowledge it.

As you do, remember to continue to remember what was stated in Message #5:

Fear is obsolete.

Know that whatever fears may be ignited by the contents of this new Message have *nothing* to do with your current level of safety.

They have nothing to do with your current level of safety.

So say to your fear, as it is said in Hawaii: *Mahalo, aloha.* Thank you and goodbye, with love.

The only safety is the safety of the light, the safety of your heart, the safety of your spirit, the safety of your soul, the safety of your godliness. Open those channels and allow that safety to be. Just be.

What in your life are you self-conscious about? What about yourself do you fear or refuse to experience or express out in the world? Let a few responses bubble up into your conscious awareness — without judgment and without censorship. Allow yourself to open. Allow yourself to be surprised.

Do you know why you are self-conscious? It is the same reason that anyone is self-conscious about anything: fear of your power.

Look into all those places in your life where you are self-conscious. Peer into the dark closets of your reluctance, the dust-filled attics of your concealment, the clammy cellars of your fear.

Are you self-conscious about your looks? Then perhaps you mask through your self-consciousness a beauty, inner and outer, that is so magnificent it frightens you.

Are you self-conscious about the words you craft on the page? Then perhaps that self-consciousness masks the immense power of your creative spirit.

Are you self-conscious about letting your voice ring out with your truth? Then know that what you fear is not another's reaction. *What you fear is your power.*

Self-consciousness is your ego-mind's protection against the very force and beauty of your power.

Again:

Self-consciousness is your ego-mind's protection against the very force and beauty of your power.

So look at those areas in your life where you carry self-consciousness and *know* that in those areas have you the greatest power.

Where are you embarrassed? Where are you afraid of being judged? These are the places where you have been judged — not for your lack of strength, power, skill and talent, but for your abundance of those qualities.

Wherever you feel somehow inadequate or embarrassed, wherever you believe that you cannot shine your light for whatever light you possess is too dim to share safely, *then it is your power you are dimming.* It is your power you are masking. It is your power you are hiding.

Jesus the Christ encouraged you to not hide your light under a bushel. Your brightest light is that part of your beingness about which you harbor the most self-consciousness.

Your light may be your voice. Your light may be your words. Your light may be your artistic and creative expression. Your light may be your inner beauty. Your light may be the soul-awakening power of your hands or your touch.

It may be any number of qualities, characteristics, abilities and capacities around which you harbor such self-consciousness that it is difficult to acknowledge them, even privately. And if you do acknowledge them privately, to express them out in the world.

Do not hide your light under a bushel. For your light shines so brightly that even through the slats of the barrel, it makes itself known. Let the power of your light break open that barrel, slat by slat, stave by stave, until your light shines through and touches everyone from your place of greatness, which is your place of greatest self-consciousness, which is your place of greatest fear.

You are the light that will transform the world. *You* are the light that will transform the world.

Know this. Act on this. Be this. For that is why you are here.

You are here to shine your light that others might feel safe to shine theirs. You are here to shine your light that others might be transformed by it. You are here to shine your light that Heaven on Earth for you and for all might accelerate.

It may be hard for you to imagine that one act of countering your self-consciousness could bring peace on Earth. But one act is all it takes. It takes but one act of empowerment, in you, for all is one and all is connected and you are connected to everyone and all that is. Your act of empowerment, however isolated, however initially private, ripples out, pulses through the energy grid of the Universe and unconsciously gives permission to others to do or at least begin to do the same.

No man is an island. You are not alone in this cosmos. This means that every other person's act of empowerment pulses to you and through you and frees you to take *your* next step, whatever it is.

Open to those areas in your life, in your beingness, where you do not feel worthy. Do it, for they are the areas of your greatest worth. And because of that, they are the areas of your greatest fear. They are the areas of your greatest power, and because of that, they are the areas of your greatest fear.

Open your heart to yourself. Open your heart to the very light that burns through you, that burns through your areas of power and empowerment, that burns through your special skills and abundant gifts.

Let your light shine. Let it shine throughout the Universe. For in this time of great transformation, in this age of great synthesis, what is needed most is the light from *your* heart, shining through you to touch others.

Shine not from places of perceived safety, but from the places of *perceived* greatest risk. These are the areas where you most greatly fear judgment, where you most greatly fear attack, where you most greatly fear destruction.

These are the areas of your power you have shut down, have *allowed* to be shut down within you — in this or other lifetimes.

Now is the time to reawaken. Now is the time to re-member. Now is the time to draw these areas of power and empowerment back to you in full force. Now is the time to draw them back to you in full force and open them up that others may be of them.

So take the area where you feel most self-conscious and befriend it, and know that therein lies your greatest power, your greatest gift and your greatest potential to transform the world.

You are safe in that, for your safety dwells not from your place of fear but from your place of strength. And these areas of great self-consciousness are the areas of your greatest strength, of your greatest gifts, of your greatest power.

Be in your power. Live your power. And through that power, contribute to the magnificent, wondrous changes that ripple through the Universe at this time. Love *all* of you. And be the power you are.

Blessings. Blessings. Infinite blessings of aloha.

7. Celebrate Your Voice

Open your heart this day to the aloha, to the love that, in their deepest hearts, all beings have for you. You are loved and, yes, protected. And for all that various parts of your body may seize up in fear, you are safe.

Parts of you may feel as though nothing has changed, as though fear still dominates your life. Parts of your body may still seize up in fear and fear may, in some ways, still seem to paralyze you.

Know this: You have come a long distance. You have come a long, noble road. Now you reach a critical intersection, a critical point of choice. It is the portal separating fear from no-fear. You *can* pass through it...*without* your fear...if you choose. If you do choose, know that it is a critical point of no return. *There will be no turning back.*

To repeat from Message #5, your fear is obsolete. It is last year's model, now discontinued. For it serves no one in the ways it once did.

Still, though you and others have traveled a long road through your fear, fear remains a core issue — for you and for all in these times of transformation and synthesis. So it is not surprising that it should arise and then arise and arise again.

In *The MoonQuest*[1], the bards — those who used their

---

[1] This first book in my *Legend of Q'ntana* fantasy series tells of a land where stories and storytellers are outlawed.

voices to sing the songs of the soul, to tell the stories of truth, to teach and love and dream and imagine, to stretch beyond what was known — were slaughtered. Their tongues were cut out. Their hearts were cut out. Their heads were cut off.

You who read this Message may have a deep cellular memory of the truth of this event...for although I present *The MoonQuest* as fiction and fantasy, it is a true story.

Many of you carry the truth of those events within you still.

Yes, you have been tortured for your words and voice. You have been tortured for your defiance.

It is time now to clear your cellular memory of those experiences. It is time now, not to let the memory of those times go as though they never existed, but to let the charge of those times go. It is time to let it go, knowing that every lifetime has its purpose and every experience has its grace.

Is it promised that no one will ever come and take you away again? Truly, no one can, with any serious accuracy, foresee or predict a future that has yet to be written.

What is truth is that you cannot go back. You cannot go back and you cannot stand still. And if there should be a physical repetition of some form of some past lifetime, then that, too, will serve its purpose and have its redemptive value. And that charge, too, can and will be released.

In this moment, what you are called upon to be and do is walk in your truth, is be the bard that you are. Be the Elderbard, as *The MoonQuest* terms it, that you are. For many are bards but few stand at the vanguard of bardship as Elderbards.

You are an Elderbard and your call now is to stand

at the helm, to speak those truths that must be spoken.

You are discovering your voice. That is the journey upon which you travel right now. You are discovering your voice. And a mighty voice it is.

It is now time to take your voice — strong, pure, vibrant, light-filled and truth-filled as it is — out into the public realm.

There are no guarantees that you will not be tortured or reviled for this — for there are no true fortunetellers.

Yet, know this: *The sound of your voice, thusly expressed, will minimize the dangers to you, not maximize them.* For every time you choose to open your mouth in power and empowerment, you are shifting the very matrix of the reality, the very matrix of the illusion, the very matrix of the Cosmic All That Is.

With each time you choose this, with each transformation that you midwife, the odds of anyone coming after you as a result of it have slimmed, for you have changed the vibration of the very cosmos.

It is time to not only walk in the fullness of your truth, to not only walk with your heart as open as you can allow it to be in *every* moment. It is time to allow *your* voice to issue from the depth of your soul and to know that as you do it, you change the very matrix of the cosmos, the very nature of the illusion/reality spectrum, the very dimension in which you and all travel.

Know that as you do this you also raise fears within yourself and within others of the consequences of these actions. Know that the purity of your heart, the purity of your soul will protect you.

Fear does not protect you. It places you in greater danger.

So transform the fear. Walk through the fear. Be the

fear in this moment and the not-fear in the next. Walk through the portal. Cross the threshold.

Do not let the fear hang about your neck like an albatross and weigh you down. Allow it its moment. But allow it only its moment. *Do not* allow it to close your heart, to shut the beauty of your beingness from the world and from yourself. *Do not.*

Shine your light in strength and in truth. Allow *that* light to be your shield and your armor.

Allow *your* light to be your shield and your armor.

It is time to clear the cellular memory of the fears that you carry. It is time.

Do it on your own or with assistance.

Do not honor your fear by clinging to it. *Do not honor your fear by clinging to it.* Let it go. Let it be. Let it be done. And move on.

You grow into a greater practice of this. Many buttons have been pushed within you — through the events of your life, through the events of your world and through these very Messages. Primal fears are being drummed out into the visible, into the palpable. Acknowledge them and transform them. Do it consciously, more consciously than you have, to date, allowed yourself to do.

Then, say as they say in Hawaii, "*Mahalo, aloha.* Thank you and goodbye with love."

Honor your voice. Honor your voice in all its manifestations. Speak your truth and allow your voice to be heard. Know that you carry a resonance and a vibration that is needed and necessary and critical to the changing matrix of our times.

Celebrate your voice. Be the Elderbard you are. And transform yourself and the world.

Namaste.

8. The Mansion of Your Beingness

Greetings and blessings, my friend. Welcome back to your connection with these words. Welcome back to the renewed energy of these new times.

Honor your courage as you move into the new after this time for you of powerful and intense transformation. Honor, too, your fortitude and your strength. Honor your love, your aloha. And honor your connectedness. Honor your connectedness with All — with All That Is and with All That You Are.

That deep, eternal connectedness means that there is no single act, anywhere in the Universe, that is without impact on every other part of the Universe. If a tree falls in the forest and nobody hears it with their ears, the tree has still fallen and the impact is still felt.

Know that.

There is no act in isolation. There is no beingness in isolation. There is no word spoken, emotion felt or expressed, curse uttered, there is no striking hand, there is no tree fallen in anyone else's presence or not that is without impact on everyone and everything.

The tiniest grain of sand being shifted the tiniest fraction of a millimeter by the tiniest breath of a breeze has an impact that ripples not only on that beach, not only on that stretch of ocean, but throughout the cosmos.

That is why it is so important that you connect with and express *all* aspects of your beingness, all places of passion within you. There are those aspects of which your conscious mind is fully aware and there are those of which your conscious mind is in fear but your Wisest Self is aware.

Let's say that today you choose to begin writing a book — or to express or deepen any other aspect of your beingness. Do not assume that simply because you have chosen to honor this one aspect that you will give up on all others.

Abandon that form of linear thought. You no longer live in a linear, one-dimensional Universe, if ever you did. Abandon that old paradigm, which is a denial of the fullness of your gifts, the fullness of your very beingness.

Of course, focus is important. But focus need not be exclusionary. Focus can be inclusionary. Several aspects of who you are can be honored and expressed simultaneous to others. None need exclude any other. No two parts of yourself need be mutually exclusive.

You will find, as you open to this way of being, that you seem to be operating so fluidly that it seems, as you might judge it, "flaky." That is not the case.

Do not judge your actions in a vacuum. Recognize that all you do and all you are is designed for a deeper purpose than that which it seems to be about. There is a surface, which is your immediate pursuit or expression. But there is the truth, which is the integration of *all* parts of yourself.

The truth is the return to wholeness.

The truth is the return to oneness.

The truth is the integration of *all* parts of yourself

— the fluidity of who you are, the multidisciplinarity, multidimensionality, multiversity of who you are...the fullness of who you are.

The focus for these times is not a mutually exclusive focus on one aspect or expression of your beingness. The focus is on your Greater Self, that expression of *all* that you are in *all* your passion and passions — whether consciously acknowledged or not.

Let your connection with your deepest self, which is your God Self and Wisest Self, align and direct your choices as you honor the fullness of all that you are.

You are moving out of a singular existence into a plural existence. You already see this in the death and outmodedness of the one-job career and one-career lifetime. It is passing from your eyes.

You are moving, instead, into a time of multidimensionality, where you will be more fully aware of the allness of who you are all the time. It is time to open more fully to that simultaneity, to that multidimensional existence, to that expression of *all* you are: a being of *multiple* purpose, *multiple* passion, *multiple* aspects and *multiple* gifts.

You were given these for multiple reasons. You were given these that you might exercise and express them *all*.

You are a multidimensional being already. You have always been. But what you are moving into is an awareness of that, an ability to exist in an awareness of that, an ability to honor and express the fullness of your diversity.

There was an expression used in Canada some years back to describe that nation: "unity in diversity." What that means is that as we move into wholeness, as we end separation and move into oneness, we will not be moving back into that same oneness from which we emerged. That initial oneness had no individuation. That oneness was just one single homogeneous glob, if you will, of energy.

Instead, we move into a higher dimension and frequency of oneness. That is what so many fail to grasp. You are not going home again, in that sense. You are rising in vibration to a higher expression of your home, which is a higher awareness of who and what you are in *all* aspects of your beingness. *That* is the power of this "Ascension."

You are moving into oneness *with* your individuality. *You* will be in unity in diversity.

Just as your fingers and your thumbs are individual, diverse expressions of the whole that is your body, so too is your beingness an individual part of the Body Cosmic.

That is increasingly the case. And what is more increasing is your awareness and your ability to be that, to be with that.

So do not hang your identity on a single peg. The coatrack of who you are has many, many pegs, just as the mansion of the Father has many, many rooms.

Your mansion, the mansion of your beingness, has many, many rooms...infinite rooms.

Each room is a different expression of your Greater Self, of the allness you are. Honor each of the rooms. For each is who you are. Honor each of those rooms. Spend time in each of those rooms.

Perhaps you have rooms you prefer over others. Perhaps it is fully justified, at times, to spend more time in those rooms. But here is the key, and this is part of the whole-making: Look into those rooms you would rather not enter, and ask yourself why that is.

Ask yourself: "What is it about this particular room, this particular aspect of my beingness, that I do not want to enter into, that I do not want to honor, that I do not want to express?"

Ask yourself.

Right now, there is a room in your mansion into which you are reluctant to enter. There are parts of you that would prefer to shut that door, lock it, throw away the key and brick up the entryway so that it is not even visible.

Do not do that.

The return to wholeness, which *is* the Ascension journey, requires that every room be visited, that every aspect of your beingness be addressed and expressed. There may be rooms you choose to renovate. There may even be old wings you choose to tear down and replace with new ones. You cannot even begin to do that if you have not spent time in those rooms and in those wings.

Your mansion has many rooms. And each room and each wing is an integral part of your beingness and *must be* acknowledged and expressed if you are to continue your whole-making journey.

It is not your conscious, physical self — your ego-mind, if you will — that will complete this journey. It is your Wisest Self, your Higher Self, your God Self, which now integrates more fully with your Greater Self, your full self.

Your Wisest Self is fully aware of all the rooms in the mansion, for your Wisest Self was co-architect, codesigner, of this very building, of this very structure.

Do not hang your identity on the peg of a single

calling, purpose or expression. You have multiple expressions, for you are a multiplicity of aspects, facets, talents and gifts.

You are here to serve in a multiplicity of ways. But true service begins with service to *your* whole-making.

For it is *your* whole-making that will ripple out into your neighborhood, your community, your country and your planet — propelling and accelerating the Ascension of every other sentient being on your planet, in the Universe and in the cosmos. For no act or choice is without impact *everywhere*.

Choose wholeness and integration. Do not trap yourself in labels. Do not lock yourself in one or two rooms of your mansion. Allow *all* the doors to remain open. Remove *all* the locks. Discard *all* the keys. Open *all* the windows, that others may know what exists in your rooms. Open the front door. Open the back door. Let your light, the light of your beingness, shine from your mansion out into the world.

You are not a one-room shack. You are a mansion of many, many, many rooms. You are a being of many, many, many aspects, facets, talents, passions and gifts — some of which you have discovered and uncovered, some of which you have not yet, and some of which you run from.

Stop running. Stop running now. Embrace the allness of all you are. Live in *all* the rooms of your mansion. Fully. Joyfully. Gratefully.

You live in times of wondrous transformation. You have *chosen* to be part of that transformation, that movement from a consciousness of the singular to a consciousness of the plural. The plural within you and the plural within all — all coming together into a wondrous [*one-drous*] oneness that remains, through its wholeness, an expression of all the individual parts, which includes all *your* individual parts.

There is no single calling. There is no one career or profession. There is no single expression of your youness. There is only the allness that you are. There is only your myriad expressions of that allness.

Do not close off any room in your mansion. Now is the time to walk through your mansion, room by room — opening the doors and windows and airing out all that stifling, locked-up energy.

Be the allness that you are. Be the mansion that you are, in this great city of connected mansions. For you will find as you air out your room that you share some rooms with others, that every mansion is connected to every other mansion. For all is one in this wondrous, cosmos in which we dwell.

All is one. Anything else is an illusion.

So shed the illusion of separation. Shed the illusion of separation first within yourself by honoring, acknowledging and expressing all that you are, by honoring, acknowledging and expressing the plurality that you are, by honoring, acknowledging and expressing the fullness of all that you are.

Honor the all of you. Be the fullness of you. Express the allness of you. Bless the multidimensional, multidisciplinary expression of you. From *that* place will you find peace — in these times and for all time.

Blessings.

Abundant blessings — of peace, expansiveness, self-realization and wholeness.

9. Choose Life

Blessings and greetings. Blessings and greetings on this wondrous day.

This is a time of reawakening — reawakening those dormant, shut-off parts of yourself. This is a time of reopening — reopening the doors of the mansion of who you are. This is a time of recalibration — recalibrating your energy field that all this may come into beingness.

This is a time of powerful synthesis, a time to remember all that you know and have known throughout the ages — from the very dawn of time to and through these end times, which are the starting times, the new times, the beginning times...the times in which you *now* live, these times in which you have chosen to live.

Yes, you have chosen these times. You have chosen them, even as many of you carry ambivalence about being here on this plane at this time.

Know that there is no binding contract to be here. It was and remains a choice — a choice you made and a choice you can rescind. Nothing holds you to this plane at this time but the deeper part of yourself, the greater part of yourself, the higher part of yourself, the wiser part of your self — your Divine Nature, your God Self — that knows and understands and *believes* in the times in which you live, in these end times, which are also the beginning times.

You made a choice. You made a choice to be here. You made a choice to participate, to carry forward all that has come before you, and to step fully over the threshold into the newness.

There is no binding contract. There are no longer binding contracts. There are simply choices. Choices made in every moment. Choices revisited in each moment to see if they remain right and appropriate choices for you.

So what of your ambivalence? Look beyond your ambivalence. Not to feel burdened by responsibility, for there is no joy in that. Not to feel burdened by the old definitions, still current, of discipline. For there is no joy in that. Not to be burdened by fear, for there is no joy in that.

Open your heart to the joy of these times: the joy of transformation and unfoldment, the joy of reawakening and reconnecting with any parts of you that have spread beyond the boundaries of your conscious selfhood.

Some of you may have entertained thoughts of departure. In this as in all, there is no right choice and there is no wrong choice. There is only choice.

From that place of choice, choose discernment. And from that place of discernment, discern the truth, for you, in these words: Choose life.

Choose life everlasting, which is the life you have now been given. Choose life everlasting, which is now the doorway that opens before you. Choose life everlasting, which is now the potential in which you live.

Choose not a life of struggle and pain, which some

of you believe you are caught in, but a life of joy, ease and infinite abundance, for that is your birthright, your divine-soul eternal right...should you choose to exercise it.

It is beyond a right. It is greater than a right. For "right" suggests that it can be taken away.

It cannot. It is an indivisible part of your soul beingness, an indivisible part that has been covered up — by fear, by the temptation of fear, by the indulgence of fear, by any number of events and emotions.

Once upon a time, at the very start of time, there was a wondrous light. A wondrous light that was All That Was. A wondrous light of love. A wondrous light of joy. A wondrous light filled with its own abundance. For it was All That Was, and so its abundance was all abundance.

Then, for reasons unimportant at present but right and appropriate at that time, once upon a time, pieces of that light began to break away. They began to break away to begin an eons-long journey of individuation, of coming to terms with the individuality that they had become.

So the years passed and the eons passed, and there was death and there was rebirth and there was death and there was rebirth. And there was karma. And there were "lessons." And there was learning. And there was pain and there was joy. And there was much fear.

Some carried such a jarring memory of that initial separation that the joy never quite returned in its fullness. Now the eons have passed and a critical threshold itself has passed, a critical threshold that, in human terms, occurred on the cusp of the millennium, during the year 2000.

At that moment, all karma was complete and all binding contracts had their bindingness canceled. And all was, in theory at least, open and free.

Suddenly, the old cycle of death and rebirth, of death and rebirth, of karma, of contracts, of what seemed like enslavement to a perpetual cycle, finally completed. You now live in the possibility of eternity. For eternity already exists. You now live in the possibility of eternity in the physical, which has never before existed for all.

The cycle of death and rebirth, of death and rebirth, and karma and contracts was a necessary program within your beingness that created the opportunity and possibility for you to cycle through the growth and the awareness that would take you to this moment of eternity.

Eternity is now...available in *this* moment.

There is a choice you can make to leave or to remain. But no longer must you leave to enter the kingdom of heaven, which what was taught for many, many generations and millennia. No longer do you need to leave.

That, by the way, was never the Christ's message. The kingdom of heaven, he said, is at hand. It is *now*. You hold it in your hand. He spoke that even then as a preparation for these times.

The kingdom of heaven is at hand. It is *your* creation. It is *your* possibility. It is *your* joy. It is for *you* to choose it.

And, yes, over the ages another way of beingness has etched certain patterns into your energy field. But like a tire stuck on the ice or in a rut of mud that seems to be spinning its wheels and not able to go anywhere, there is a way to change the pattern.

For the car, it is a rocking motion, which frees it from the rut...a very appropriate word. For you, it is a choice, a choice supported by energetic restoration. Choose to reactivate and restore what once was, in those moments before the light that was All That Was began to separate and individuate into individual souls, into individual beingnesses.

Choose life, life eternal, life everlasting.

Choose no longer an enslavement to fear, which has been the cultural and human pattern almost since the moment of splitting off. Restore, instead, the original pattern, not from a place of homogeneity, but from a place of individuality. Make that choice.

You are not a rising to some cloud dressed in white where you will play harps for the rest of eternity. That is not what the kingdom of heaven is. The kingdom of heaven is at hand, at your fingertips, in this lifetime, now. And you can choose it. You can choose to choose it in every moment.

You can choose to choose abundance. So choose it.

You can choose to choose joy. So choose it.

You can choose to choose love. So choose it.

You can choose to choose an end to fear. So choose it.

You can choose to choose a body that is such a paragon of health that it will carry you for as long — in tens, scores or hundreds of years — that you would choose to have it as your Greater Self's vehicle for experiencing all that is, in *all* the dimensions.

You *can* make that choice. So choose to be here. Now. Not in your fear and not in your despair, which is a lack of hope. But in your joy. And in your abundance. And in the very truth and knowingness of your beingness. Choose now. Choose life.

Allow the patterns of fear that have instilled and installed themselves in your soul energy grid to shift back into wholeness, to shift back into completeness, to shift back into the perfection of joy and love.

Yes, it is possible, though perhaps in a theoretical sense, for you to make that complete shift in this next breath. But for most embodied on the Earth at this time, it is a journey. It is a process.

It is a voyage not of discovery but of *re*discovery, not of awakening but of *re*awakening, not of changing but of *re*-membering, of reattaching all that has been dismembered: the limbs of your highest beingness — the joy, the love, the passion, the abundance and the wholeness in all respects with which you are coded.

The codes for all that lie within you, lie within your energy field, the energy matrix of your soul, the energy matrix of your Greater Beingness, your Greater Self.

Your Greater Self encompasses the fullness of all that you are, expressed and still yet unexpressed — both the part of you that was the light that broke off from the Great Oneness of light and the part of you that has, already, returned to that light, though you do not yet fully know or feel it.

Your soul was coded for eternity. But that soul encompasses every part of you, and so *every* part of you is coded for eternity — your physical beingness no less so than any other part of you.

There are many ways to reactivate and restore your original soul energy pattern, to reawaken those codes that have been crusted over by limitation and fear. There are many ways to break down the pattern of fear and reweave the fabric of your essential beingness. There are many ways to do this and many beings who can do this, including you, from a place of love, from a place of fearlessness, from a place of aloha.

Use your discernment to determine which is appropriate for you at this time. One powerful means is through the use of energy and vibration. Energy *is* the new medicine: sound, light, vibration — for that is what you are, vibration. Energy is the truth of what you are. Why would you use anything but energy to work with energy?

There are, of course, other modalities, transitional modalities. Again, use your discernment, for all carry the potential to contribute to the wholeness and wholemaking of this cosmic nation, of this Body Cosmic.

Reawaken to the truth of your beingness. For in that reawakening and in the knowledge of the truth will you know how best to serve *all* of your beingness, which is, in its potentiality, eternal.

Open your heart to yourself and know that all healing comes from within you. Open your heart to yourself and know that return to wholeness is *your* choice.

Make that choice. Make the choice now to return to the perfection that is yours. Make the choice now to launch or continue your sacred journey of reawakening, re-awareness and reemergence. Make the choice now to recognize the light, not only that you are but that all are.

Make the choice now. And in making that choice, know that all other choices will flow and fly from that. Make the choice now.

You are already well-embarked.

You are already well-carried forth.

You are already on a path of alignment.

It is that very path of alignment within you and within so many that causes what some term the forces of darkness to seem more present and ominous.

Make the choice for light within yourself. Make the choice for life eternal within yourself. And all that apparent darkness will fade, in time. Make the choice to be and see and acknowledge and embrace all that you are — the full oneness that *you* are. And in doing so, the full oneness that is All That Is will once again be embraced in this world.

Make the choice. Choose not ambivalence. Choose commitment. Commit to the fullness of who and what you are, now and in every moment. Embrace it lovingly. Embrace it abundantly. Embrace it undeniably. And see, as you lift the restrictions on your beingness, how you lift the restrictions on your ability to attract to you all that you would desire in your heart to live the life that you would choose.

There is no for cause for fear. So choose life. Choose a life devoid of fear. Choose a life filled with joy and aloha. It *is* within your power to do it. Make that choice. Make it for yourself. Make it for all.

You are love. That *is* what you are. You are love and you are loved. I love you, each and every one of you, with the same love that I call upon you to feel for yourself and each other.

It is not a love that is encircled and enclosed and restricted by conditions and conditioning. It is not a love of limiting emotion. It is a frequency and vibration of wholeness, recognition, openheartedness, aloha.

I leave you in that field of aloha and invite you to remain in that field throughout your day, choosing it with each breath, moment by moment, breath by breath, nowness by nowness.

Choose life, life eternal. Choose love, love that embraces all creation. Choose optimism. Choose joy.

Choose to be the fullness of who and what you are in every instant, in every moment, at every level.

Free yourself from the shackles of your fear. Transform those shackles into the brilliant light of your freedom, which is the radiant brilliance of your love, your aloha.

Aloha, dear friend. Aloha and namaste.

10. Your Rainbow Self

Greetings, my friend. Greetings and blessings on this fine day. Today is a day to address the illusion of duality...the illusion of a black-and-white world where all that is "good" is white and all that is "bad" is black... where there are "absolutes" that unequivocally define every moment of existence.

There are no absolutes. There is no uncompromising judgment. There is no unyielding "guilty" or "innocent," "good" or "bad," "dark" or "light." There is no black-and-white.

The only truth is what lives in your heart. What lies in your heart is neither black nor white. It is all the in-between. It is the shadings. It is the colors. It is the hues...the rainbow hues of your beingness.

It is fear that has created this illusion of duality. Yet even fear is not black-and-white. There are fears that protect us still, but there also fears that have served their purpose and are no longer required to keep us safe.

How do we distinguish between them? How do we navigate the infinite shades of gray that lie between black and white, darkness and light?

Discernment.

Discernment is the most consequential tool you have as a light-carrier and Way-Shower. It is your compass on moonless nights, your astrolabe on stormy seas, your pilot through the maze of fear, doubt and uncertainty every human must travel. It is the powerful torch that shines brightly but mercifully into the darkness all carry within.

The torchlight of discernment exists that you might see and acknowledge your own darkness — not for you to attack it for the enemy it is not, but that you might embrace it, love it and transform it...that you might change its form into something that better serves your evolution and humanity's.

The job of light-carrier and Way-Shower is rarely easy or straightforward because any time you raise the light in yourself, you also see what lives in the darkness.

Yet darkness is not evil. It is not the "black" in a black-and-white world. That world exists only in your mind. It is not real. Thus is it time, again, to move away from the duality of black versus white, dark versus light.

All is. That is all.

Has darkness arisen for you, within you? It has and does for all.

When it does, do not turn your face from it and declare it to be "bad." Look upon it. Ask it what it has to teach you, what it has to show you, what it has to demonstrate to you.

Once you see and acknowledge what that is, then that darkness is free to be released...is free to change its form into something else.

Your darkness does not seek to hang about. That is not its chosen task or mission. It lies within you waiting to be freed.

Enslave it no longer. Enslave *yourself* no longer.

Allow the light to shine through you. Allow it to bring up those bits and pieces of darkness that sometimes seem much larger and more daunting than mere bits and pieces. Allow the darkness to speak to you, that you might know what within you is ready for trans-formation.

You are a wondrous creature, a wondrous creation, a wondrous being of great depth of light.

Within you is also harbored darknesses. That is nothing to be embarrassed or fearful about. That is to be acknowledged.

Know the fullness of who you are — light and dark and all that lies in between.

For the days of black-and-white have passed. It is time now to embrace the full color range, the full color spectrum of your beingness.

Choose to embrace it. Choose to embody it. Choose to transform and transmute any and all that does not serve your highest good in this moment. And now in this moment. And now in this one. Choose from your heart.

What do you choose to create in your life? What would bring you joy in your life? These are not always simple or easy questions. For many, sometimes, the most difficult thing to do is to delineate what it is that their heart desires.

What is it *your* heart desires? Open to that. Open your heart to that. Open your mind to that. Not from a place of enslaving responsibility or enslaving service. Nor from a place of fear. Service is not about fear. Service is not about joylessness. Service is about joy. There is no service in joylessness, for there is no modeling in joylessness.

Let your heart sing. Let your heart rejoice. Let your heart love. Let your heart be. Through that beingness, allow yourself to feel *all* that would move through you, that does move through you, that *is* you.

Bring *all* of you back together again. Bring it all back together again and reconnect with the fullness of who you are — in every dimension and on every plane of existence, all of which exists in a simultaneity that your mind cannot yet grasp. But there it is. There it is.

Open your heart to yourself. Open your heart to all aspects of yourself. Allow them to reveal themselves to you so that all that does not serve you in this moment can be transformed.

Your journey, the Earth's journey, is one of trans-formation. A changing of form from the old to the new, from the three-dimensional to the multidimensional. From the single plane to the multi-plane. From black-and-white to a color spectrum of infinite colors, hues, shadings...and frequencies, for color is nothing but frequency.

That multicolored, multidimensional reality is the true beauty of the Universe...the true beauty of you. That is what it is time for you to move into.

So transform the blackness of your fear — not necessarily into whiteness, but into the infinitely multicolored energy spectrum that you are. Do that, that you might experience and express the fullness that you are.

In one moment that fullness can include your fear. In the next, having seen it and acknowledged it and paid homage to it for its past service, you can transform it into something else, something that does *now* serve you.

Go now into your day. Experience the multicolored palette that you are, the shadings and hues, the darker colors and the lighter colors — all coming together in a brilliant, radiant oneness.

Love yourself.
Honor yourself.
Celebrate *all* that you are.
Blessings. Abundant blessings.

11. Speak Your Truth

Greetings, my friend. Greetings and Namaste. On this day, the message is simple: Speak your truth. Speak your truth, though all that you fear would rise up to stop you. Speak your truth, though all within you would silence it. Speak your truth for that is your savior.

You still believe, at times, that your fear will protect you. You still believe that by holding back you will be safe.

Know this: There is no safety in holding back. Even Salman Rushdie[1] came out of hiding when he realized that. There is no safety and there is no hiding. Not anymore. Not for you. Not for anyone on a conscious path of integration, whole-making and re-membering.

You may not, even now, know the fullness of your truth. That is okay. Open your heart. Open your heart as wide as you can, then wider still.

Then wider still.

Open your heart not only to share your love and your truth but to receive it. How can you be a clear vehicle for truth if your heart is closed? So, open.

Open and trust.

---

[1] British author Salman Rushdie went into government-protected hiding after Iran's then religious leader, Ayatollah Khomeini, issued a *fatwa* or death sentence against him, claiming that his 1988 novel, *The Satanic Verses*, was blasphemous. Although the *fatwa* is still in force, Rushdie is no longer in hiding.

You fear? Transform your fear. Fear has no place in your mansion at this time. [See Message #8.] Go into that room, that room that is your fear. Go into that room and begin a thorough cleaning and clearing. Acknowledge the fear and then open the windows wide and allow the fresh breezes off the ocean of spirit to blow your fear away.

Transform your fear. Change its form to joy. Change its form to heart.

Speak your truth.

You don't yet know the fullness of your truth? Then write. Write not what you think you know. Write to discover what you know. Write to discover the truths that lie deep within you, truths that have lain hidden — even from you.

It is your fear that has kept them hidden. Transform your fear and feel those truths rush to the surface with a force you did not know you possessed.

Speak your truth. That is the only way to peace. That is the only way to love. That is the only way to oneness. That is the only way to the Heaven on Earth you came here to midwife.

That's right. You came here to midwife a dimensional shift and planetary transformation so wondrous that you cannot yet grasp the fullness of it nor the import of it. Yet that is what you are here to contribute to.

You do it. You do it well. There is more to do. And that "more" is the fuller, clearer, louder, more vocal, more passionate expression of your truth. At all times. In all ways. At all costs.

Yes, at all costs. There is no more time to fritter. There is no safety curtain to hide behind. Unless you step forward with your truth, there will be no Heaven on

Earth. The cosmic transformation will cease its journey of unfoldment, and the Armageddon of Separation will be the only alternative.

Speak your truth. Whatever that truth is — be it about peace, love, oneness, All That Is — that is the truth that yearns to be spoken.

Walk the Earth naked, clothed only in your truth. Do it and do not fear the nakedness, for your truth is the only protection you now need.

Perhaps things were different in the past. But the past has passed and now it is time to walk fearlessly and defiantly into the future with nothing between you and the world but your truth. Express it as you will — through the spoken word, the written word, the painted canvas...whatever. Take *your* gift of truth-telling — you *do* possess it — and throw open the shutters of your fear and hesitation.

Speak it. Express it. **Be it.**

There is no time left to leave it unexpressed.

You have a book percolating in you? Write it. Write it now. Do not wait for some perfect moment. There is a message you need to express? Speak it. Do not wait for some perfect moment.

Do it now. In whatever form it calls upon you to employ.

Times *are* urgent.

You stand at a crossroads, an intersection between the high frequency of empowered love and the low vibration of fear. Do not give in to the low vibration. Allow yourself to resonate to the highest amplitude you believe you are able to manage. And then higher still.

You are the peacemaker. You are the Way-Shower. You are the leader. You are the priestly class whose example *will* change the world, *will* change the course of history…if you choose to act on your soul's imperative.

Speak your truth.

Speak it for all to hear. Speak it regardless of perceived consequences. Speak it as though your life depended upon it. For it does. Not only your life, but all life.

You think this an exaggeration? Look around. Read the headlines. Fear is the currency of the times. It is time to devalue that currency into extinction. There is no room for it, no place for it, no time for it.

Speak your truth. Only you know what that means for you. Open to that truth. Trust it. Know it with all the knowingness you possess. It is time. It is time to know and be known.

Forget past years of criticism, bullying and judgment. Forget past lives of persecution and torture. *They do not matter now.* They do not exist now.

All that exists is *this* moment. This moment of truth. *Your* truth.

Speak your truth. You cannot hear that mantra often enough.

In the days and moments between this writing and your reading of it, it will be yet more critical.

Do not seek what you *believe* to be true and truth. Seek what you *know* to be true and truth.

Go within. Go deep within. Allow that truth to emerge in whatever way it must. Allow it to emerge. And once it does, launch it out into the world. Launch it with the force of your power and empowerment, the force of your love, the force of your passion, the force of your commitment.

You made a choice to resonate with the frequency of

higher truth. Now you have no choice but to act from that frequency.

Express that truth, your truth. You either know it already or you are coming to know it, in bits and pieces. *Do not run from it.* Even as it shocks or frightens you. Even as it tears away parts of you that you believed to be unchangeable. *Do not run from it.*

This is the time of knowingness, of surrendering to the great, vast and glorious knowingness that you possess, the great, vast and glorious knowingness that is the all that is of all *you* are.

Open to it. Open to it, acknowledge it and surrender to it. Trust it. Know that it alone has the power to save and protect you, to serve and nurture you.

Let *your* truth set you free. Let it break apart the shackles, burn down the fortresses, flush out the hiding places and throw open the prisons that have held you back, held you down, disempowered you and fed off you.

Speak your truth. Climb to the tallest tower, the highest mountain, and shout it from the heavens of your beingness out into the world. The world needs it. The world is ready for the transformation it will herald, even as parts of the world would struggle from it and with it.

Think how *you* struggle against parts of it. Think it only for a moment then let it go.

You are the light of the world. That is your call and your calling. That light is your truth. Shine it. Shine it so that all may hear, so that all may grow and transform from your modeling of it.

Be the courageous empowerment that will change the world, transform the Universe, free the cosmos.

Be it. Be it now.

Now is it time to rekindle, reignite and renew that eternal flame of knowingness and truth, to shine it out for all to see and know.

What is *your* truth? Own it. Speak it. Free it.

Let it find its way through the neurons of the energy grid of the cosmos into the hearts of all, even those for whom your message would, at first blush, seem anathema. They will soften. Their hearts will soften. For if yours softens, theirs cannot help but do likewise. How can it be helped when all are one?

Speak your truth. Trumpet it from the rooftops with aloha, and *know* that **there is no other way.**

12. Own Your Voice

Aloha, my friend. Behold the God-light within you. Behold the Source flame within you. Behold the christedness within you, the Buddha-ness within you, the power within you.

This is a power you have yet to fully acknowledge and embrace. Breathe into that power in the certain knowledge that it is there waiting to be reignited, waiting to be rekindled, waiting to find once again its full expression through your beingness.

You are the light of the world. You are the light of your world, which is all the world, which is all the cosmos, which is All That Is.

Shine your light. Think of a dimmer switch on a lamp or light. Do you realize, at this moment, how low you have set that dimmer switch, that rheostat? Do you realize how brightly you can turn that dial or push that lever so that the light that you are is magnified and amplified so wondrously that it touches the hearts of *everyone*?

You ask how to bring about peace? Begin by bringing peace to your own heart. Bringing light to your own heart. Amping up the energy of peace and love, of peace-making and lovemaking, in your own heart.

You are a being of such immense power, of such immense strength, of such immense fearlessness that were you to be faced with that power, strength and fearlessness in the mirror and could see it fully, you might not believe it was you.

It is.

It is.

It is.

It is time at this time to embrace more fully who you are, to embrace more fully your power and empowerment, to embrace more fully your strength and your light, to embrace more fully your voice. Your voice for peace. Your voice for love. Your voice for truth.

Are you afraid? Are you afraid of the consequences of what you might say, of what might issue from your lips should that voice be given full and free rein?

Know this. Know it as surely as you know the fingers on your hand, the hands on your wrist: The greatest danger that exists for you and for all — physically, emotionally, spiritually, cosmically — is the danger of silence.

To you who have been silenced too long, to you who are exercising your voice but not to its fullness: It is time to own your voice, your voice for truth. [Message #11 spoke to this. Consider this an amplification.]

It is time to open the floodgates of truth-speaking and truth-seeking that lie within you. Open them, for in so doing, all the darkness that now engulfs you and the world will be flooded with light. For the power of your voice *is* the power of light. And the power of the darkness that you struggle so much against — in your life, nationally and globally — is the power of silence.

This is not about speaking reactively. Many now do this with great ease. A button is pushed, something is triggered, and we speak out. That is not speaking truth. That is reacting from a place of fear, hurt and defensiveness.

When the call comes for you to speak your truth, to open your voice, to allow the truth to cascade from your lips as the greatest of Niagaras, that call relates to the truth of your soul, the truth of your heart, the truth of peace, the truth of oneness. That call has nothing to do with the angry railings of fear, bitterness and revenge.

Vengeance is old. Vengeance is dead. Vengeance begets more vengeance, which plunges the vengeful farther from the light of their christedness and deeper into a darkened hellishness of their own creation.

The truth of these time is, as the Christ spoke, the truth of love and wholeness. That does not mean that there is no anger. What it does mean is that underlying any anger must be an energy of love and peace.

You are here to make the peace, to re-create the peace that you have torn asunder. Whatever lack of peace that has been created in the name of so many great teachers can be dis-created. As in alchemy, it can be turned from lead back into gold — the golden light of peace, truth and love. These are not trite words, as tritened as they have become.

These are more than words. These are vibrations that increase the frequency and resonance of your beingness, of your planet, of the cosmos.

Speak your truth. Speak the truth that only *your* soul knows. Speak the truth that your soul would speak through your heart were it given free rein.

Open the connection between your heart and your throat.

Imagine, if you will, a road that runs between the energy centers of your heart chakra and your throat chakra — a line of energy that links the two. Such a line of energy does exist. Imagine it. Imagine it now.

Imagine yourself traveling that road from your heart to your throat. Is it a straight line or does it meet roadblocks, detours, ambushes? Notice what blocks the voice of your heart from finding expression through the very place of expressiveness in your being, which is your throat.

There are many, many, many avenues for truth-making. It could be a vocalization of your truth, a writing of your truth, a painting of your truth, a music-making of your truth.

Open to those avenues that are perfect for you in this moment, knowing that as you open to them more fully, others will emerge to demand an opening.

Open the line of energy between your heart and your voice. Open to it. Breathe through the blocks and barriers. Breathe through the fears and reluctances. Breathe through them all and transform them into the power of your will and the power of your voice.

Speak your truth, gentle soul. Speak it, express it, fully, powerfully, with the fullness of your power. Do not hesitate for a moment. And do not permit anything within or without you to still your voice.

Be in *this* moment with your voice. Be in *this* moment with your truth. Be in *this* moment with the power of your heart. The power of your heart that is so forceful and so force-filled, so broad and inclusive and expansive, that it embraces and enfolds all that is — light, dark and every hue, color and shading in between

Do you already allow words of amazing grace and power to flow through you from a seemingly outside source? *There are no outside sources.* All lies within you.

Perhaps you have been "channeling" this being or that being, sending out amazing messages of light and hope and truth and love and peace. Know this: You move into a time where it will be not only important but critical to lay aside the separation between yourself and the beings that you "channel."

Now is the time of integration. Now is the time to allow whatever beings' energies that speak through you to become more fully a part of you and to speak with your own voice under your own name.

The time approaches for you to own *all* parts of yourself under the umbrella of your current beingness. The time approaches to lay down the crutch and mask of another name and to be the truth of *your* words out in the Universe.

You no longer need to go into trance or semi-trance to communicate the truths that you do communicate, that you have been communicating, that you will communicate. You do not need to go into trance to be connected. A trance is disconnection from the *allness* of All That Is. It connects you with a higher part of yourself but *separates* you from the world.

Open your eyes as you open your heart and your mouth. Claim all parts of you. Claim the Melchizedek you are. Claim the Quan Yin that you are. Claim the Mother Mary that you are. Claim the Christ that you are. Claim the Archangel Michael that you are. Claim the God that you are. Claim *every* part of who you are.

We are all one. Every name mentioned already resides fully within *your* heart. *In* your heart. *In your heart.*

It grows time to claim your heart.

That does not mean you do not have a connection with Melchizedek or Mother Mary or Quan Yin or the

Christ or the Buddha or Mohammed. It means that you no longer need to separate yourself from that energy. It means that you and that energy are one and the same. It means that your voice and your name are what are coming to be needed to ring through the land.

It may not be today. It may not be tomorrow. It may not be next week. And it may not be next month. But it is coming. When it does, open to the possibility of speaking *your* truth with *your* voice, with *your* name, calling on all the energies of the Universe to support you — and being conscious.

The world needs strong voices now, voices that speak not only to the converted, not only to those who are in alignment with the "name-brand" messenger. The world needs voices who speak to *all*. It is from that allness, that inclusiveness and that oneness, that all will come together again.

Allow it to come together again in *your* heart now. Then watch as that embrace, that oneness, that inclusiveness, spreads across your nation, around the planet and throughout the cosmos.

If you are separate from the Christ, if you are separate from Melchizedek, and simply allow them to "work" through you, how are you not separate from your neighbor, your partner, your child...your enemy?

All is oneness. Embrace that oneness through the embrace of your power and all that you are.

Open to your power. Open to your voice. Open to your light and your love. Open to the fullness of who and what you are. Open to it now and in every moment.

You are the light of the world. Let your voice ring through the world. Let your voice carry that light. Carry it on your own power. Carry it on your own name.

The Book of Messages

Perhaps that name is not the name you now carry into the world. Perhaps there is another name by which you need to be known now. Open to that possibility.

Open to that possibility, knowing that you carry many, many sacred, holy, spiritual and vibrational names through your life and lifetimes. Each is an expression of your soul at any given moment[1].

Open to that. Know that when you speak from the place of truth that is who you are in this moment, that it may involve a different name. That does not mean hiding under a different name. That means opening to a deeper, more powerful part of yourself that has its own expression in name.

Begin by opening first to your soul, the heart-voice of your soul, the expression of your power through your heart. Trust that. Be that.

Align with the oneness that is the truth of All That Is.
Align with the love that is the truth of All That Is.
Align with the peace that is the truth of All That Is.
Align with the heart that is the truth of All That Is.

As you do that, the Heaven on Earth of the whole-making journey that you travel draws close enough to consciously experience.

The Kingdom of Heaven is here. It is in your hand. Now. As you open to your soul and the heartful truth of it, you will allow it to emerge, to appear, to come into focus, for yourself and for so many others.

Remember this: Every heart opening, every opening to truth, every voice opened in truth and peace and love,

---

[1] Over the years, I have been known as "Mark," as "David," as "Akhneton," as "Aq'naton" and, now, as "Mark David." Each name has expressed an aspect of a soul that is greater than any single name can describe...the right and perfect aspect and soul expression for that moment in my life.

is a whole-making not merely for the speaker, not merely even for those who hear or read those words. It is an energetic opening in consciousness for the entire cosmos.

You have a responsibility that transcends your beingness. For your beingness is but a part of the oneness of All That Is. And as you bring into focus those energies within your beingness, you help give permission to others to open to it in theirs.

Do that. Do it today, whatever day it is that you hear or read this. Do it today, this day. Commit to speaking your truth. Find a way to honor that in your day, in your beingness.

If you wish to change the world, if you wish to bring peace to the world, bring it first through the power of the peace of your own voice and heart, your voice expressed through your heart. That is the truth.

So this day, this *moment*, open your heart to the truth that lies within it. Open your throat and your voice to the expression of it. And begin to open to the possibility of owning that more fully in your own name, whatever name is the name that calls for it to be owned by.

Now is the time to wish you a wondrous, truth-filled, love-filled, peace-filled day, expressed fully through the fullness and source of your beingness.

Love the love that you are. Love your voice. Love your truth. Love your ability, your power, your imperative to change the world.

Go in peace. Go in love. Go in the power of your voice to change the vibration and the frequency of your life and all lives, of your planet and all planets, of your beingness and all beingnesses.

Aloha.

Namaste.

13. Choose Empowerment

Greetings. Greetings and blessings on this new day of your empowerment. Greetings and blessings on this new day of your deliverance from the weakness of your fear, the uncertainty of your mistrust and the shakiness of your uncertainty. Welcome. Welcome. Welcome.

This Message follows in natural sequence Message #12, which discusses how important it is to step into your own empowerment and your own voice, to claim that empowerment and voice, and to allow for the integration within you of all that, which and who have moved through you in the past.

Now is the time, in this Age of Synthesis, for that integration to occur, for you to *choose* for that integration to occur. For it is your choice.

To that end, it is important for you to know that these are no longer, strictly speaking "Messages from Melchizedek[1]."

Melchizedek energies inspire, inform and underlie every word. Yet in keeping with the call for integration that was a theme of Message #12, the God Self that is the Higher Self and Wisest Self of Mark David Gerson now claims authorship *and responsibility* for these words.

In effect, what is coming through in this Message

---

[1] When the first of these Messages was distributed in late 2002, it bore the heading "Message from Melchizedek."

and all Messages is the energy of the highest self of Mark David Gerson / Aq'naton Ben-Isha Yoseyva[2], *into which has been integrated the energies of Melchizedek*, those same energies with which he, with which I, with which we — with which you — are so greatly and so fully aligned.

Is this still "channeling"? Yes, in a manner of speaking. And no. For the words that emerge through these Messages are not the words of ego-mind or personality mind. These are words and concepts that flow from Highest Mind — words and concepts that emerge from a deep, conscious connection with heart mind, soul mind, spirit mind and Divine Essence, all of which embrace *all* those beings and energies, including Melchizedek, that are in alignment with the God Self of the being currently embodied as Mark David Gerson.

You, too, can choose to integrate the energies and beingnesses that have moved and spoken through you. You, too, can choose to integrate them and say, "In the oneness of All That Is, I *am* All That Is. The entire Universe, the entire cosmos, dwells within me and projects out of me, as do all energies."

Make that choice. Choose to begin to begin to begin the process of such integration. Whether or not you believe yourself to be channeling this being or that, begin to focus on *your* highest self, *your* wisest self, *your* Greatest Self, *your* God Self. Begin to deepen that connection, for *that* is the source of your strength, your power and your light.

Your ego-mind/personality self is but one *small*

---

[2] In 2002, when the original Messages came to me, I was using the spiritual name Aq'naton Ben-Isha Yoseyva — both in my writings and out in the world. I returned to my birth name in 2005. I write about those name changes in *Acts of Surrender: A Writer's Memoir*.

part of the *greatness* that you are, which encompasses, embraces and enfolds into it *all* that you are.

It is time to enter into a place of connection and connectedness with that greatness. It is time to act and speak from that place, knowing that, in so doing, you empower yourself to speak not only with the voice of Melchizedek, Quan Yin, the Christ, Archangel Michael, Archangel Gabriel, Archangel Ariel, Mother Mary or your dolphin brothers or sister, but with *all* of them in alliance and in combination and in complete integration within your Greater Self, the Greater Self that is the truth — energetically and spiritually — of who and what you are.

This is the Age of Synthesis. This is the Age of Integration. It is an age not only of bringing back all those parts of you that have been flung aside or hidden. It is also the age of bringing in those parts you refuse or are reluctant to claim ownership of. For some of you, Quan Yin resides powerfully within you. For others, it is the Christ. For others still, it may be the Buddha or Melchizedek. All these reside within *you*. And it is important now, in this time, to begin to claim that part of you. To not say, "Oh, I channel Melchizedek. So I take no responsibility for the words that come through me." Or, "I channel Melchizedek, so I don't have to think, because this is not me." Or, "I channel Melchizedek, so I don't even have to know or be aware of what is coming through me."

Statements such as those are not part of your empowerment. And anything that is not part of your empowerment is part of your *dis*empowerment and thus not part of your greatest good.

Empower yourself. Claim *all* that you are. Claim your

Buddha-ness. Claim your Melchizedek-ness. Claim your Christ-ness, your Mary-ness. Claim your Quan Yin-ness. Claim all the loving energies that have ever moved through you. Claim them and integrate them *now* into your beingness. And allow yourself to receive them from a place of consciousness.

The days of going into a deep trance and being unaware are drawing to an end. The days of being in a high vibration *only* when in meditation are over.

There is no time or space or place for unawareness. What moves through you — be it the energy in your hands as you perform Reiki, the energy in your voice as you do a sound activation, the energy in your words as you speak or write, the energy in your heart as you open in meditation — all of these are part of *you*.

How can it not be when all is one?

When the cosmos and the Universe are all one, how can they not be? And so it is time to begin the process of claiming them back.

Quan Yin resides in *you*. Jesus the Christ resides in *you*.

And every time you acknowledge that reality within yourself, you open to the possibility of others acknowledging that within themselves.

That is what being a Way-Shower is all about. It is not about shouting, "Follow me!" It is about living the truth that is the light of your Greatest Self, living it with joy, living it with love, living it in public, living the fullness of your capacity in each breath and in each moment, knowing that on many levels, it then affects each and every one in this cosmos.

It affects them energetically, because we are all part of the same energy grid and your empowerment *rockets* through that grid to touch everyone else in that grid, igniting a spark within them that allows them to do the same.

It empowers them, too, because you become a role model. As you walk the Earth in your new empowerment, your frequency and vibration — the very means of your beingness — shift and change. And anyone, *anyone*, who comes into contact with you, in even the most superficial way, cannot help but be altered, shifted and transformed by your new energy. And so they begin to experience *their* transformation, and on and on it goes.

This is an age of wondrous transformation. You are a part of that...to the extent that you empower yourself.

Take back your power. That doesn't mean grabbing it from someone and disempowering them. It means claiming *your* power *for* yourself, not your power over someone else. It means claiming back for *your*self the power you have abdicated to others.

Open your heart *and* mind, to the greatness that *you* are, a greatness that encompasses and embraces all the great masters and teachers who have ever worked with you or through you in this and all lifetimes, in your conscious awareness or otherwise.

This is the Age of Synthesis. Take them into you. Take them in and then speak with *your* voice and *your* name, thereby creating an opening for all to do the same.

It is time now to embrace your voice and power, and to embrace them publicly, to put them out into the world.

If you resonate with these words, with these Messages, then you already resonate with Melchizedek, then the energy that *is* Melchizedek has worked with you and spoken to you and through you in the past. Perhaps it has done so without you even being aware it. There are likely already ways in which you act, speak or do your works of healing and whole-making that are Melchizedek speaking and working through you.

Now is the time to acknowledge that, not to give your power to an energy that carries a name different from your own, but to acknowledge that at all times, when you are in your power, you personify and exemplify and model and embrace not only Melchizedek but all the energies of *your* beingness, of cosmic beingness and cosmic awareness.

Message #12 encouraged you to move out of trance when you do your deepest work. Your call now is to be conscious at all times. To be awake and aware at all times. To hear and *know* the words that move through you. To move into a growing consciousness. So if now you operate in trance, begin to move into a place of at least semiconsciousness. And if now you are semiconscious in your words or your work, begin to move into a place of full consciousness.

These are *your* words. This is *your* healing touch. The sounds you make issue from *your* mouth and *your* voice. It is time to own them. Not from an ego place of "better than," but from a place of knowingness and empowerment that opens *all* to the beauty and truth of All That Is, which is all that *you* are.

It may not be easy to surrender to this imperative. But there are occasions on this cosmic journey of heart-opening, transformation and self-empowerment when we are called to speak and do things that are not easy, that are not comfortable.

Your comfort zone is your place of disempowerment. There is no comfort zone. Your comfort zone is that place where you stop being the fullness of who you are, where you cease transforming, where you cease removing yet more blinders from your eyes and yet more filters from your light.

There is no comfort zone.

There is only the voice of your heart, the voice of your Divine Essence, which *is* the voice of God. For God is within *you*. That is why these Messages use terms and phrases like God Self. God is within *you*.

All resides within you. And all is possible from that place. All *is* possible from that place.

I love each and every one of you. I honor each and every one of you. I open my heart to each and every one of you, particularly to those who struggle with these words. All I can say to you is, "This is the voice of my truth and my spirit. This is the voice of the integrated Melchizedek-ness within me calling out to you to be of the oneness that you are, to, again, love all the parts of that divine nature, that Divine Essence."

Now is the time to be a channel for *your* highest self, for *your* Greatest Self, for *your* God Self, for *your* Divine Essence. Now is the time, not to disappear into trance, but to *be* that channel in all ways and at all times. Now is the time to open that connection, to keep it open in consciousness. Now is the time to awaken and re-member, reattaching and reintegrating those "members" that have become dis-membered, unattached. Now is the time to re-member all of the parts of who you are, the greatness of who you are, to re-member it, to reawaken to it, to reintegrate it and to be it.

Do not reserve your Melchizedek-ness for whatever

channeling or whole-making work you do. *Be* your Melchizedek-ness in all moments and at all times. *Be* your Christedness in all moments and at all times. That is what it means to be conscious.

That is why it is so important to move away from the idea of trance, from the idea of being enlightened *only* in moments of meditation. Now is the time to be consciously aware, to be open, to be the light that you are in all moments, at all times, in all ways and in all words. Now is the time to make that choice moment-to-moment to the best of your ever-increasing ability.

Now is that time.

Once again, know that you are surrounded by and embraced with great love, with great aloha. Once again, fill yourself with the certainty that you are a being of infinite power, infinite light, infinite aloha, infinite strength, infinite ability and capability.

Open to *your* heart. Listen to *your* spirit. Claim *your* Divine Essence. Claim it in all you do. Be it in all you are. And know that from *that* place, all that is good and glorious, all that is abundant and free, all that is truth and true, all that is light and love, all that is the oneness that you are, will express itself to you and through you in a fullness you have not yet even begun to imagine.

Infinite blessings to you on this journey. Abundant blessings to you as you travel the road of your empowerment.

You are Melchizedek and Melchizedek is you. You are Jesus and Jesus is you. You are God and God is you.

Acknowledge that within yourself and be the empowerment that you are.

With this breath.

And now this one.

And now this one.

The word "Namaste" is a recognition of the God-essence, the divinity within you. Recognize and acknowledge it within *yourself* — now and in every moment.

Namaste, dear friend.

Namaste.

You and Melchizedek

I am no more "connected" than you are. I am no more intuitive than you are. Nor have I been gifted with exclusive access to Melchizedek energies. They are available to you right now and in every moment that you open your mind and set your heart to it.

The key is to abandon the fear-based controls that keep us locked in a prison of logic and unbelief. The key is to remember the truth of our infinite nature. The key is to listen, trust and surrender.

If you have read any of my *Way of the Fool* books or my books for writers or have attended any of my workshops, you will recognize elements of my Muse Stream technique in what follows. The Muse Stream isn't the only way to touch that inner realm where our Melchizedek energies reside. But it is a method that has proven effective for my students and clients over the years, as well as for me, so I am happy to share it with you here.

To quote from my book *The Voice of the Muse: Answering the Call to Write*, "Write and let the words flow from your pen onto the page. Write and let the spirit of who you are emerge onto the page. All those things will happen the moment you unlock the gates that have kept the words, ideas, thoughts and feelings dammed up inside you. The Muse Stream frees you to allow that flow to happen. How? By training you to keep writing — through doubts, hesitation, fear and (seeming) unknowingness."

Seeming unknowingness? Absolutely, for the Melchizedek connection you seek has never left you and never will!

Free Your Melchizedek Energies onto the Page

These are guidelines, not rules. Adapt them in whatever way feels most relevant and appropriate. Simply remember that the goal is to let go all control of the process and to trust your intuition and inner sensings, both in terms of how you approach the experience and how you view the results.

Have pen and paper, tablet or laptop handy, or sit as comfortably as you can at your desktop computer.

Settle into a physical, emotional and spiritual state of stillness. If you have a meditation practice, do whatever you normally do to get into a receptive space. If not, close your eyes and sit quietly, focusing on your breath to quiet your mind. Use music, aromatherapy, crystals, yoga or ritual if you find any or all of these to be helpful. You can also use the "Step Into Your Melchizedek Energy" meditation later in this section to both relax you and guide you through the experience. (If you are unable to still your mind, don't worry about it. Writing your mind chatter will give it voice and, ultimately, silence it.)

The key to getting your "message" is to write without stopping, to write without thinking, to write without correcting spelling, punctuation or grammar, to write without censoring or second-guessing, to write through and past any judgment or fear, to write in a morning-pages, stream-of-consciousness sort of way... to write on what I call in my books for writers the "Muse Stream." I call it that because when we surrender to the experience unconditionally, the words pour through us as effortlessly as water in a free-flowing stream.

How do you start? Here are two options...

- Write the first thought that comes to mind. It can be a question or feeling. It can be a statement of praise or complaint. It can be the voice of your inner critic, your fear or your inner child. It can be nattering mind noise. Whatever it is, write it, then let a response emerge spontaneously onto the page. Don't look for an answer. Don't think about an answer. *Let* the answer. The answer is your "message."

- Write: "I open my heart to the Melchizedek energies within me and listen for their message for me in this moment. The message begins with a single word, and that word is..." Continue with the first word that bubbles into your conscious awareness, then write on the Muse Stream from there.

Should you get stuck, simply repeat the last word or sentence you were able to write freely and keep repeating it until the flow returns. It will. Also, refocus your attention on your breath: If you are stuck in this exercise, you may be stuck in your breath.

For your first experience with this exercise, set a timer for at least twenty or thirty minutes. If you feel able, keep going for another five or ten minutes after the timer goes off. With subsequent experiences, write for as long as you feel the need to and then a little longer after that. The wisest words and deepest truths often emerge after we think we're done.

If, when you're finished writing, you feel doubtful, cynical, judgmental or mistrustful of what has emerged, don't read it right away. Instead, set your "message" aside for at least an hour. Take a walk or do something else unrelated to this experience. Then, when you feel able to look at what you have written uncritically and without judgment, read it with an open heart and mind to discover what messages your Melchizedek energies have for you.

Read more about the Muse Stream in any of my books for writers.

Step into Your Melchizedek Energy: A Guided Meditation

Record this meditation for playback, get a friend to read it to you (and then return the favor) or get into a quiet space and read it to yourself slowly and receptively, following its directions and suggestions.

If you prefer a professionally guided approach, I have recorded a version that is similar to what follows. It's titled "Meet Your Muse" and it's one of the tracks on my album "The Voice of the Muse Companion: Guided Meditations for Writers." Here's how to access it:

- *Stream the individual track or the complete album for free as a subscriber to Apple Music, YouTube Music or Amazon's Music Unlimited.*
- *Download the individual track or the complete album from Amazon or Apple Music.*
- *Download the full album from my website.*

Relax. Close your eyes. Get into a comfortable position. Let your shoulders drop. And drop some more.

Take a few deep breaths, breathing in calm and quiet, breathing out fears, fatigue, stress. You're relaxed but alert. Awake and aware. Moving into a quiet place. A deep place. A place of freedom, openness, vision, awakening.

In your mind's eye, see a door. A beautifully crafted

door. Handcrafted. A work of art. Perhaps it's a new door, newly discovered. Perhaps it's ancient, as old as time, simply waiting for you to rediscover it.

See it or sense it...however you see it or sense it.

This is your doorway of inner vision and inner wisdom. Walk up to it. Run your hand over it. Feel its texture...its richness...its depth.

As you touch the door, it swings open. The door to your inner wisdom and inner vision will always swing open at your touch...if you let it.

You are the key.

Now the door swings open and you step across the threshold. Into a wondrous place. Perhaps you recognize this place. Perhaps it's new. Whatever you see or sense and however you see or sense it is perfect, perfect for you, in this moment.

See or sense this place, this wondrous place. See or sense it fully, using all your senses. What does it look like? What colors do you see? How is the light? Do you hear any sounds? Smell any smells? Reach out and touch something. Feel its texture. What is the spirit of this place? What does it feel like, to you?

Now, coming toward you through this wondrous place, coming toward you bathed in light, is a representation of your Melchizedek Energy...an energy that lives inside of you...an energy that is not separate from you...an energy that is the essence of your oneness, your wholeness...an energy that embodies the integration of all aspects and parts of you...an energy that embodies your unique, individuated contribution to the greater whole of all Creation, to the Cosmic Oneness, to the Divine Wholeness and Holiness that is All That Is.

This representation could show up as a person or

other being, as a celestial body, as a disembodied or insubstantial color, shape or light, or as something else altogether. However it manifests, whatever you see, sense or feel of it, is right for you. In this moment.

Open your mind and heart. Especially your mind. And allow this representation to come to you in whatever form it comes, recognizing that its form can change from moment to moment and mood to mood. It can change, too, from one experience of this meditation to another.

There is no right or wrong image, right or wrong way. There is only the way you see or sense, and what you see and sense. And it's perfect. For you. Right now.

What does your Melchizedek Energy look like? Feel like to you?

See or sense it fully. Again, use all your physical senses — sight, touch, smell, taste, sound. And your intuitive senses — feeling, spirit, essence.

Your Melchizedek Energy now stands before you, and you greet each other in whatever way feels right, taking all the time you need.

Now, you and your Melchizedek Energy begin a special exchange.

Perhaps your Melchizedek Energy has a message for you. Perhaps you have questions for your Melchizedek Energy — questions about a specific issue or situation in your life, questions about how you are feeling or wish you weren't feeling, general questions about your day or your life, or questions about anything at all.

Your message may show up as words. Or it may show up in another, nonverbal way. Be open to whatever comes up and however it comes up. Let the experience go where it will. Let it take you where it will.

Take thirty seconds of silence for this exchange. Transcribe it if that will assist you. If you choose to write it down at this time, pause the recording until you're done. As you write, remember to remain in the flow of the experience by writing without judging, censoring or second-guessing, without stopping to correct, without stopping for any reason.

Now that you feel complete with that interaction, step forward. Take another step. Then another, moving closer and closer to your Melchizedek Energy...until you step into your Melchizedek Energy, until you and your Melchizedek Energy become one, merging in a wondrous moment of divine union...merging into an accurate representation of what your Melchizedek Energy is: an indivisible part of you.

What does that feel like? What sensations or emotions run through you? What do you see? Sense? Hear? Intuit?

Breathe deeply into the merged entity you are and experience all there is to experience...feel all there is to feel...be all there is to be.

Take twenty seconds of clock time to experience this fully.

Now that you feel complete with this part of the experience, know that your Melchizedek Energy resides within you all the time, in every moment of every day... even when you are not consciously aware of its presence. Know, too, that you can call it back in to your conscious awareness at any time. All you need to do is remember its constant, full-time presence. All you need to do is remember how it felt to be here and how it felt to be connected to it. All it takes is stillness. A quiet time. A quiet place, where you're free to envision, where it's safe to connect.

Now, turn back to the door — that special door — knowing that you can return to this place at any time. You can return at any time for a more conscious "meeting" with your Melchizedek Energy or to connect with any other aspect of your Greatest Self.

Once more, you touch the door, it swings open and you step through…and back.

As you return to your starting place, you bring back with you all that you sensed and all that you saw and all that you heard, felt and intuited. You're bringing it back to your conscious awareness, remembering whatever, in this moment, it serves you to remember.

When you're ready, but only then, open your eyes, staying with all you experienced.

Write about it — what you saw, felt or sensed. Write about any message or messages you received. Write whatever you remember, whatever comes up, taking all the time you need.

Remember to keep your pen moving across the page. Remember to breathe. Remember to censor nothing, freeing the voice of your Melchizedek Energy to live through you on the page.

Gratitude

It has been a journey of nearly two decades from the original edition of *The Book of Messages* to this one, and there have been many people over the years to whom I owe a debt of gratitude.

My first thanks, however, precedes that initial copy-shop version and must go to all those around the world who followed my "Messages from Melchizedek" when they were merely emails and online posts: It was the depth of your response that sparked that first edition.

My gratitude reaches farther back than that, though, to a time before I even knew the name Melchizedek. I could never have opened up to those initial messages and to so much more in my life without Carole H. Leckner, who, in helping me awaken to both my creativity and my spirituality, taught me to trust the voice of my deepest inner knowingness, without Jeremy Emery, whose child's heart nudged open the doors blocking mine, and without Mary Omwake, whose *mana* inspired me to choose love.

To them I must add a special shoutout to Lee Graham, sadly, no longer physically present among us. Sedona's premier metaphysical networker when I arrived in town in 1997, Lee "adopted" me almost immediately. My Sedona life and all that flowed from it — including, ultimately, my Melchizedek connection — was richer and fuller for Lee's presence.

This edition of *The Book of Messages*, not to mention some of its predecessors, could not exist without the support and encouragement of a far-flung group of friends whose belief in the depth of my vision and the power of my words has never wavered. These include Adam Bereki, Joan Cerio, Sander Dov Freedman, Aalia Kazan, Kathleen Messmer and Karen Weaver.

To my students and coaching clients over the years: Your spiritual and creative courage has never failed to ignite my own. As such, your energy is also very much a part of this book.

Thanks, too, to the spirits of the lands I have journeyed through and trod upon over the years, many of which have directly or indirectly fed *The Book of Messages* in its various incarnations. Among the most significant are Nova Scotia's Yarmouth and Kings counties, which midwifed *The MoonQuest*, my first book and the one that would make all my other books possible; Penetanguishene, Ontario, where I first penned messages such as these; Maui, where so many walls around my heart shattered; Albuquerque and its Sandia Mountains, where the 2014 edition of *Messages* was birthed; and Sedona, where the energies of Melchizedek first identified themselves to me and which has called me back to it to work with them again.

Nearly two decades ago, I concluded the first edition's acknowledgments with a thank you to my daughter. I do so again: You are as present in my heart and as much of an inspiration to me as always. And I still love you all the way to the moon...and back.

More from
Mark David Gerson

Acts of Surrender: A Writer's Memoir

Changing Channels

Some might describe the *Dialogues with the Divine*-style writing that entered my life in Penetanguishene as "channeled." I did too, initially. But as I grew to see writing as a co-creative act not as something separate from the writer, I dropped the term. Here's how I would later put it in *The Voice of the Muse*: "Even the most conscious act of creation is not yours alone. Nor is the most unconscious act totally separate from you. There is a quantum oneness that's always at work."

During my first Sedona sojourn, however, I continued to explore the traditional channeling I had experienced in Boise. Early in 1998, I took a channeling class and discovered that I had a gift for it. More accurately, perhaps, I was deepening my gift of surrender and learning to own my voice and trust it. I had always been too frightened of other people's judgments to risk speaking up or speaking out. Even in school, I was not a hand-raiser and rarely participated willingly in open discussions. That was why I had always preferred math with its single right answer to English class. I had moved past much of that fear by the time I participated in Helene Rothschild's Sedona channeling class. Still, it felt presumptuous to announce to the group that I had just received a message from Jesus. Earlier, Helene had guided us into a meditation to help us connect with whatever entity or energy was ready to speak through us. Afterward, we would be free to share any message we received.

Timidly, I raised my hand.

"Akhneton[1]?" Helene nodded at me.

My knees shaking but my voice strong, I shared both what I had heard and its source. A few moments' silence followed. Did no one believe me? Finally, a fellow student spoke up.

"Oh, my God," she exclaimed. "I saw Jesus too. He walked in this direction and I thought he was coming to me." She looked at me. "Then he walked right by me and went to you."

However exciting and validating it felt to be channeling celebrity entities, it rarely worked that way for me. Even in those early *Dialogues*, the Divine never identified itself. When I asked for a name, the response inevitably would go something like this: "I am part of you. Yet I am apart. I am love. I am truth. As are you. We are one." For someone as insecure as I was, such answers were not helpful. For someone learning deeper levels of trust and deeper levels of truth, they were perfect.

Our one-room flat at the Hunters' was cramped for two adults and a toddler, but its location at the edge of the National Forest land that surrounds Sedona more than compensated, at least for me. Most mornings, often before Q'nta and Guinevere woke up, I would slip out for a hike. Sometimes, I would carry a pen and pad, park myself on a rock and dialogue. More often, I would take our portable cassette recorder and channel as I walked. It was on one of the latter days that I found

---

[1] Akhneton is a variant of Aq'naton.

The Book of Messages

myself speaking a message so unlike any I had ever received, in both tone and content, that I insisted on a source. The name that I sensed was Melchizedek.

The Biblical Melchizedek is a king and priest who first appears to Abraham in Genesis. In metaphysical circles, he symbolizes a powerful source of ancient wisdom. Hearing the name Melchizedek that November morning was nearly as startling to me as channeling Jesus had been four years earlier. When I felt pushed by that same energy to make this and future Melchizedek messages public, I was just as reluctant.

After a few weeks' resistance, I surrendered. I emailed that initial message to a small selection of friends, clients and students, encouraging them to pass it on. Within two days, I had received more than forty requests to be added to a Melchizedek mailing list — all from strangers. Within a few months, the email list had mushroomed to more than six hundred people in twenty-five countries, and the messages were being reprinted on metaphysical websites around the world. Some months after that, I collected the first thirteen into a self-published volume titled *The Book of Messages*.

If the early messages were popular, the thirteenth, titled "Choose Empowerment" and distributed four months later, was less so. In it I was urged to drop Melchizedek from the "Messages from Melchizedek" subject line and claim ownership of and responsibility for all the words that flowed through me. It didn't matter how those words showed up; they were all part of me now. In the email accompanying number thirteen, I explained that future messages would carry my name, not Melchizedek's. Not all subscribers were pleased. Some, missing the self-empowering, integrative point of all the messages, viewed Melchizedek as a more trustworthy source. Others took issue with two of the message's urgings: that readers stop going into trance when channeling ("there is no time or space or place for unawareness") and that they stop separating meditation from the rest of their life ("your call now is to be conscious at all times"). Little did I know that before long, two other of number thirteen's declarations would propel me into the next phase of my spiritual journey: "It is now time to embrace your voice and power, publicly… out into the world" and "You are God and God is you."

Be inspired! Get your copy of Acts of Surrender *today from www.ActsofSurrender.com, Amazon or your favorite bookseller.*

Dialogues with the Divine: Encounters with My Wisest Self

Foreword

The "dialogues" in this book emerged from the silence and solitude of a fiery autumn and frozen winter. I had just moved a hundred miles north from Toronto to the rural outskirts of Penetanguishene, a summer-resort town on the shores of Lake Huron. For the fifth time in two years, I had packed my few belongings and followed my heart along the asphalt road of my soul's journey.

Why was I there? If I needed a reason for the world, it was to work on my novel, *The MoonQuest*. Whatever else materialized, I hoped that a fourth draft would. After all, *The MoonQuest*'s earlier drafts had been largely written during just such a time of retreat.

Although *The MoonQuest* was a constant theme during those five months, I made little progress on it. Instead, even as I struggled to move the novel forward, other words came, and I soon found myself being propelled on an unexpected journey of healing through writing.

Mine was a heart-sickness — neither physical nor life-threatening. But it was soul- and spirit-threatening. For without trusting that it was safe to let the world more fully into my heart and my heart more fully into my words, I could never take my writing and life to deeper levels, never fully live the precepts I taught in my seminars and workshops.

I have always seen creative writing as a metaphor for creative living, believing that the principles that work for one unfailingly work for the other: faith, trust, surrender and openheartedness; vulnerability, truthfulness and flow. And, of course, being in the moment.

Opposing all of these is fear.

If fear no longer paralyzes me, it still occasionally slows me down. It's the core issue of our time, triggering everything from writer's block to war. It's the only barrier to flow — of words, of abundance, of life, of love.

Many layers of fear had dissolved for me by the time I installed myself at 296 Champlain Road two days before my forty-second birthday. But more healing awaited, as it always does.

Opportunities for growth arise out of every breath when we are open to them. Often they arise most clearly when we step into the stillness. For me, this place of stillness was a sparsely furnished one-bedroom flat across the road from the spirit-filled waters of Georgian Bay. Sharing my rear wall was a larger house, home to Angela and Jim Emery and their nine-year-old son, Jeremy. Jeremy instantly adopted me and my cocker spaniel, Roxy, and his outpouring of unconditional love was among the first challenges — and opportunities — of this journey. Others followed in rapid succession, relating as much to my life as to my writing.

Meditative or inner dialogue is a technique I have often taught in my writing workshops. Once in a meditative state, you ask a question and then allow the answers to emerge through what I call "writing on the Muse Stream" — setting pen to paper or fingers to keyboard and letting the words flow through you onto the page, without stopping for judgment, censorship, editing, correction or second thoughts. Whether you believe the answers come from God, your Muse or a deeper part of yourself, they do come...when you let them.

My first written words of that five-month retreat came as inner dialogue, though not one that my conscious mind had initiated. Instead, as I sat in meditation one morning, I heard the words, "I just want to say something." It was an echo of a recent nightmare and when I engaged it in conversation, I discovered a part of me that I had unwittingly denied.

By mid-January, these occasional dialogues were surging out of me, sometimes two or three times a day, and "dialogue with the divine" had replaced "inner dialogue" as the heading in my journal.

Generally, the first words of dialogue came the moment I closed my eyes. When that happened, I reached for my pad and, eyes still shut, recorded what I heard, sensed, experienced. More often than not, the power of the words evaded me. At times I resented them. In that respect, I was no different from my writing-workshop participants who, when writing for the first time from a place of heart and truth, often reject their work as meaningless or pedestrian. It wasn't until later, as I typed and read over the day's writing, that I began to sense its transformative power.

Through this ongoing dialogue and the experiences that sparked it, I began to open my heart wider and wider still, to trust deeply and more deeply still, to surrender more and more completely to a wisdom and divinity I had never before acknowledged. Through them I began to embrace more fully my vision, my power, my strength and my truth. Through them I began to discover new ways to write, new ways to teach, new ways to live, new ways to be.

I had set out to write a different book. I tried to write that other book. Instead, this one appeared — not initially as a book, but simply as an outlet for all that floated into consciousness.

Who is the Divine? What was the presence I engaged when this book spilled out of me? It is the presence that resides in all of us...the light that shines in and through each of us...the presence that infuses everything and everyone at all times and in all ways. There are many names for it: Muse, God/Goddess, Infinite Mind, Great Spirit, Higher Self or, as I put it in the book's subtitle, Wisest Self. In short, it is the Divine, part of each of us and all of us, yet at the same time something of which we are all part.

Who was I speaking to? Who was speaking to me? That still small voice that is not really small at all. It is the largest, deepest, truest part of ourselves, if we but open to it, honor it, embrace it, choose to accept its oneness with us. That is the Divine who came to me — to whom I opened the totality of my being in order to access and receive these inspiring words. That is the divinity we all share, the divinity we can all touch as we write and live.

My dialogues with the Divine began out of need — not the need to write a book, but the need to reconnect with my wholeness and my heart. I share them with you now, knowing that my words are your words, my fears are your fears, my strength and courage are yours, as is my love and wisdom. For we are all one beneath the skin of individuality. We are all one in the divinity and divine presence of love.

Who is the Divine? It is you, me, God, the flowers in your garden, the trees in your yard, the kitten that cuddles on your lap as you read these words. It is the very words themselves. May they move, guide and inspire you as they did and still do me. And may you move from them to your own direct links with your own divinity.

Be inspired! Get your copy of Dialogues with the Divine *today – from www.markdavidgerson.com/books, Amazon or your favorite bookseller.*

Be the Melchizedek You Are!

Let Mark David Be Your Guide on *Your* Melchizedek Journey!

- Spiritual Coaching & Mentoring
- Writing/Creativity Coaching & Mentoring

It's time to reignite your passion!
It's time to realize your potential!
It's time to rekindle your dreams!

Book Your Session with Mark David *TODAY!*

www.markdavidgerson.com/contact

Sessions are available in person
or remotely via Zoom/Skype/FaceTime

www.ingramcontent.com/pod-product-compliance
Lightning Source LLC
Chambersburg PA
CBHW030152100526
44592CB00009B/240